Street Girl

A life of hardship, heroism and hope

For you
with
love
xx

PWM
PEN WORKS MEDIA

STREET GIRL

First published in June 2016 by
Pen Works Media Ltd
54a The Broadway, Crouch End, London, N8 9TP

This book is a work of non-fiction

www.penworksmedia.co.uk

Marketed and publicised by Gilmara Prates

Printed in England by Clays Ltd, St Ives plc

ISBN: 978-1-908730-16-9

For my mother, who gave me her work ethic;
For my father, who gave me his dreams.

CONTENTS

PROLOGUE

MY FATHER WAS A DREAMER. He would tell stories and dance the samba, the lambada and the xote gaúcho. He would go for long walks into the worlds he invented for himself and then, when he came back, he would talk about the people he met. To a young girl like me, his stories were enchanting. I would sit and listen, wide-eyed and intoxicated.

This is one of those stories:

There was a beautiful woman who lived in a field of sweet potatoes. A fresh-water stream ran close to the field and there was a mill with a big wheel where the woman ground the sweet potatoes into flour. The woman loved to dance while she was making bread from the flour and anyone who smelt the bread would want to dance, too. People passing by would be filled with lightness, just like the sweet potato bread. They would begin to dance – the samba, or the lambada, or the xote gaúcho.

Many people heard about the beautiful sweet potato dancer, but no-one ever saw her. They would go into the big field to search for her and call out to her, but she'd just disappear. Some said she was a young woman who fell in love with the moon and was heartbroken by the fact she couldn't reach up to it. One night, she saw the reflection of the moon in the water of the stream and fell in while trying to embrace it. She became a water spirit, her body taking liquid form and becoming as elusive as the ripples, currents and sparkling little splashes of the stream.

Still she made the bread, and so sweet was the smell that I wandered into the sweet potato field. I began to dance, round and round, for hours. The beautiful woman was so impressed that she appeared and danced with me. We danced together through the night and I awoke the next morning by the side of the sweet potato field.

Often I returned to the field and, every time, I danced with the sweet potato woman. People would follow me, hoping to catch sight of her, but they would only see me dancing through the sweet potatoes.

One day, a rich plantation owner approached me and asked how he could meet the sweet potato woman, as he too wanted to dance like her. Your father is a poor man, Rozana, and the plantation owner offered me a hundred reais for the information. I told him the woman was in love with the moon and that if he went to the field at night, disguised as the moon, the sweet potato dancer would appear to him.

That night, the rich man went to the field carrying a bright candle, hoping the woman would mistake it for the moon. But, instead of finding the sweet potato dancer, he came upon Boitatá, the serpent with the horns of a bull and huge eyes of fire that slithered through open fields after nightfall. Boitatá saw the candle, mistook the man for a firefly and swallowed him whole.

He was never seen again.

Over time, many men came to the field to dance with the sweet potato woman, but nobody ever found her – except me. This is how I became the best dancer in Brazil.

Guess what, Rozana? The sweet potato woman fell in love with me and forgot all about the moon. She asked me to marry her and go live with her in the watermill, but I was already married to your mother, so I had to say no. The sweet potato dancer asked me again and again, every time I smelt the bread and came to the field. She said she would turn the watermill into a wonderful palace made of silver, gold, mother-of-pearl and precious stones of all kinds. I would never be poor again!

It didn't matter. I kept telling her I couldn't marry her, but that I would go to the field and dance with her every night. She was sad, *but accepted the arrangement. So, every evening after work, I would take the long walk to the sweet potato field. I would dance all night and wake at the edge of the field each morning.*

By now, your mother grew suspicious of me being away every night. People came to visit our home and asked where I was. When your mother said I'd gone on one of my walks, they would reply, "Are you sure he's not with the sweet potato dancer?"

Rozana, this annoyed her very much.

One night, she decided to follow me to the field. She smelt the sweet potato bread and your mother too began to dance. She looked so beautiful and I danced with her. We danced and danced and we looked so well together. The sweet potato woman saw us and realised that all the gold and precious jewels in the world would never be able to come between our love. She told me there was no need to keep coming to the field every night. I was already the best dancer in Brazil and there was nothing more she could teach me.

So I came back home and, every night, instead of going to the sweet potato woman, I would dance with you.

I always wanted to be able to dance as well as my father and I asked him, when I was young, if I would ever meet the sweet potato dancer. He said I might, some day, if I was out in the fields and I smelt the bread. If I was good, she might appear to me and teach me as she taught him all those years ago.

Through the years, I often smelt that sweet potato bread, faintly, coming from somewhere far away. I smelt it when I was hungry, when I was down with depression, when I thought about killing myself, and when I was being held prisoner, repeatedly raped and tortured. The smell came to me through the darkness and seeped into my soul.

But I never saw the sweet potato dancer.

Until now.

Street Girl
A life of hardship, heroism and hope

ROZANA McGRATTAN

with *John F. McDonald*

CHAPTER ONE
CRACOLÂNDIA

São Paulo was known as the 'city of rain' – and I remember it falling on me then. The rain. Not heavy, like the worries on my mind – just persistent and stubborn, and it was getting cold.

A chill wind blew up from the south. It touched my heart and made me shiver. Winter was coming, it was wet and I was homeless.

Again.

The only clothes I had were the ones I stood up in.

The sun was shrouded overhead, unable to break through the thick cloud cover that surrounded it. The light was translucent, like in an impressionist painting, with objects in the foreground moderately in focus and the distant vista hazy, with soft outlines blending into each other.

I started to walk through the teeming streets, not really knowing where I was going or what I was going to do – moving slowly through the city centre and watching the illegal street *mascates* run away when the police came. Most of the people were migrants from the north of Brazil or from Colombia, who came to São Paulo for a better life. However, without skills or an education, they couldn't get jobs and soon ended up in poverty, living from glimmer to glimmer in the hope of finding some luck.

Despite my predicament, I was hungry, and even the smell of despair couldn't contaminate the aromas from the street cafes and food stalls that came at me, curling and cajoling round my nostrils. I had very little to eat that day. I intended to buy breakfast on the way to work in the morning, but now all that money was gone – stolen – and I'd been thrown out onto the street with nothing.

I had been homeless before, but not in a city as big or as violent as São Paulo. I wondered why I'd come here in the first place. Should I not have gone back to my village and returned to my family? For a moment, the longing came back, but deep down I knew there was nothing there. That's why I left, to drift to Ponta Grossa, then travel to Imbituva and Maringá, and now here, to the largest city in Brazil. Besides, I'd burned all my bridges several times over.

There was no way back.

I thought about going to Edifício Copan, to the flat of the eighty-five-year-old man who hugged me when I was robbed and bought me a pizza. I slept with him and asked him to marry me, but going to him wouldn't have been fair. I'd hurt him once when I put the key he gave me through the letterbox and never came back. I didn't want to hurt him again – or bring trouble to his door.

I thought of going to the office where I worked, but I'd only just started there and what would they say if they found me lying on the floor in the morning? Or sleeping in the street outside like a lost dog, my face cut and bruised where Olga had punched me?

Night was falling and there was nowhere for me to go. Gradually, the enthusiastic streets emptied of workers and were replaced by the night people – drunks, thieves, drug-addicts, pimps and pushers. Sirens constantly squalled past like excitable harridans and doormen from the buildings hulked about hump-backed in the shadows, looking for sex from homeless girls like me.

It was a dangerous place during the day, but at night it was hostile, angry and treacherous. I tried to sleep in the well-lit doorway of a city-centre bank, but the security guard woke me. When I wouldn't let him have sex with me, he moved me out onto the dirty wet pavement, where I eventually closed my eyes. But it was a fretful sleep, constantly disturbed by the sounds of the city night and hooded spectres leering past me in the lecherous neon-light.

I don't know how long I'd been sleeping when I was woken by a street boy. He was short with dark, matted hair and weather-rough brown skin. He was as dirty as an old shoe and wore a torn T-shirt and shorts. He must have been cold in the night-chill and could not have been any more than eight-years-old, half my age. He asked me for money.

'Do you think I would be here if I had money?'

He smiled. His teeth were black and broken, like mine used to be. He told me it was a dangerous place to sleep. I could be raped or killed, or even worse, picked up by the police.

'You should come with me.'

I was so desperate that I did.

His name was Hiago and it was just beginning to get light when I followed him to a place in the south-west of the city centre, known as 'Cracolândia.' It was an area in the Luz region of São Paulo that was very affluent in the 1960s, with plush hotels, theatres, shops and restaurants. Only the very rich lived there. It stretched from Republican Square and spread to São João Avenue through to Luz Station, which was built by the British – who taught the Brazilians how to play football.

Now it was populated by the destitute homeless and the once five-star hotels, theatres and cinemas had long since degenerated into porno palaces, frequented by perverts and prostitutes. The people in this place were all crack addicts – hence the name.

Crack is a drug that has a short-lasting high, so everybody was always on the edge, constantly waiting for their next fix. It was a graphic place with people shivering, wrapped in dirty blankets, or slumped on damp, stained sofas and old mattresses, or just lying on the bare pavements.

Entire families floated like flotsam on a rat-infested sea of sadness. Most of them looked dazed, shuffling along in a psychotropic world with glazed eyes. Their dirty faces were repeatedly illuminated by flashes of fire as they smoked a mixture of crack cocaine residue and anything else they could find – like crude hemp or tobacco –

openly from makeshift pipes.

Hiago told me there were about two thousand homeless people there, but nobody could say for sure because they came and went, or died or got killed or taken away to be tortured by the police.

I wondered how I would be safer here than in the city centre, as it looked like a much more dangerous place. The boy took me to a group of kids whose average age was about thirteen, with the oldest being no more than eighteen. He said I could be one of them – a street girl – and they would take care of me. I was skinny myself, but I looked healthy compared to these kids. They were random arrangements of small muscles and bone, held together by leathery skin. They were gathered in a square with some trees and concrete benches and tall buildings all around. They eyed me up and down suspiciously.

'Hey Hiago, who is this?'

'I found her on the street.'

They were mostly boys, but there may have been a couple of girls as well. It was difficult to tell. They were androgynous in their mutual squalor and emaciation. Reluctantly, their names crept towards me – Luiz, Tiago, Rosangela, Damiao, Ronaldo, Dilma and a few others that I no longer remember – and I walked with them through the zombie-like denizens of Cracolândia.

Some people were fighting and screaming at each other. Mothers of young children were weeping and wailing. It was by far the dirtiest place I had ever seen, every street filled with filth and faeces and piles of stinking rubbish everywhere. People vomited, defecated and urinated openly all over the place and the smell almost choked me. It wasn't just the place that stank, but the people too. Most of them looked like they hadn't had a bath in years, and they'd been wearing the same old stained clothes for just as long.

I'm not sure now what month it was – maybe May or June – but it was almost winter and cardboard huts were springing up everywhere – behind trees, in shop doorways, under bridges and in abandoned buildings.

People were searching through big municipal garbage containers for scraps of food, or gathering up the discarded fruit and vegetables left over from the street markets. Others were begging from the early-morning passers-by who tried to ignore them as they hurried along, almost running in their eagerness to get past the tattered tramps.

The place was infested by insects of all kinds – mosquitoes, beetles, flies and maggots crawling everywhere all over the ground. I could see rats and dogs scavenging for food and the water came from fountains that people washed in during the warmer months. But now, in the wet winter, everybody looked dirty and dark-skinned and toothless. It was difficult to tell the age of an individual because the intensive use of crack residue made them all look so much older than they actually were.

My sleep outside of a bank on the previous night was fretful, but on my first night in Cracolândia I didn't sleep at all. Children as young as five walked around with heavy hand guns. People were smoking crack residue until they fell to the ground in convulsions. Anybody who was foolish enough to venture down here on foot after dark was attacked for a few *reais* so the kids could get their next fix.

The pungent stench of crack cocaine was everywhere, like burning plastic, and it stung my eyes with its acidic haze until I cried tears of ammonia. The group I was with split empty drinks cans to light the stuff and they had makeshift pipes to smoke it from. Whole families were addicted. Generations eagerly awaited their next fix. It was a legacy of sleazy languor passed down from father to son; mother to daughter.

I watched as police made a few token excursions into Cracolândia, just to prove to the newspapers they were doing something about the place. But they just beat people up for fun, kicking them and sometimes killing them. Who was going to complain if a crack-head got crippled?

Nobody.

Middle-class boys drove past in their flash cars and threw petrol bombs out of windows, setting fire to people who ran round screaming as they burned. Children as young as two and three were sexually assaulted with their parents' consent for money to buy crack. Women were raped and beaten until they were unconscious, and I saw one girl give birth on the dirty ground surrounded by flies and maggots; nobody to care for her or help. I felt compelled to go to her, but Hiago stopped me.

'It would be a mistake, Rozana.'

'Why?'

'You must not get involved. There is too much pain here. If you get involved, you will be overcome by it all. You must become immune.'

'But you helped me.'

'Did I?'

The next day, I thought about going to the office – but how could I? I was dirty and bedraggled and I smelled of the streets. The shoes Stephanie loaned me after I got robbed had been stolen, too. I had to stay there for now, until I got my bearings.

In return for their protection, the group decided to test me. They didn't give me a choice. I *had* to go along with them. We went picking pockets, like Fagin's gang in Oliver Twist, which I read when I worked on a pig farm for food and lodgings. The woman there had a lot of books.

The older boys in the gang attacked and robbed any lone person they came across in the side-streets and alleyways. They had pre-planned escape routes through the maze of the slums, over fences and across derelict areas, should the police come.

I didn't know how to pick a pocket so Hiago told me to watch him do it. Because I was a novice I had to help create a diversion, bumping into the target or falling to the ground in front of them, pretending to faint, getting into a fake fight with another gang member, or crowding round the target while they crossed a road.

Sometimes we got nothing. Other times, we got a few coins or, if we were particularly lucky, a wallet or a watch. The ones the bigger boys beat up would be stripped of everything – their clothes and trainers and anything else they had, anything that could be traded for crack. It was risky. The boys would use a gun or knife to frighten the victims, but there was always the chance the victim would be armed themselves and then someone would inevitably get killed or seriously hurt.

The sad thing about it was, most of the people the group robbed were just ordinary workers on a minimum wage who had to pass through Cracolândia to get where they needed to be. The rich and the middle-class were kept safe in gated communities and apartments in the more salubrious areas of the city. They only came near Cracolândia when they wanted to burn people for fun after a party.

Let me be clear, I didn't want to be part of this robbing and stealing. I've always abhorred violence of any kind and I always felt sorry for the victims. At the same time, if I hadn't gone along with it, I would not have survived.

Almost everybody in Cracolândia was addicted to crack cocaine. It was an epidemic. People came there looking for friends or relatives who had disappeared and they ended up addicted themselves. There was a constant, fluctuating population who fell prey to the local drug dealers.

Children as young as four and five could be seen smoking the pipes and I knew they would never reach adulthood, but nobody cared – not the police, the politicians, the church, nor the general public. We weren't regarded as people. We were vermin, on a level with the rats and the maggots we shared our living space with.

The newspapers constantly called for the place to be burned to the ground or bombed or blitzed, along with all the people in it. The government would have gone along with it too, if they could have got away with the genocide.

For many others, though, Cracolândia was a place of convenience. Most of the high-level dealers who sold their merchandise in the area lived outside it and it was an expedient place, for the most part safe from police attention, to ply their trade. Police took bribes from the dealers and politicians took bribes from the police. The news magnates sold their papers with lurid stories that the safe people liked to read, making them thank their lucky stars they didn't have to live in such an awful place.

This, in a way, made Cracolândia useful to everyone, not just the unfortunate addicts imprisoned there.

It wasn't long before I came into direct contact with the drug trade. The São Paulo gangs sent in their poison to a "leader" who would make us kids distribute it. You couldn't say "no," or you would be shot. We would never be paid for our work, but given crack for our own use. However, I was old enough to see the dreadful effects of the drug and so I promised myself I would never use.

I never believed I'd be a permanent fixture of Cracolândia, like my friends. I somehow knew I'd find a way back out, so I never sank down into the soothing despair of the drug and managed to keep away from it. The rewards the dealers gave me always went to my friends, who only used this crack residue as it was the cheapest of narcotics, and all they could ever afford.

The dealers would come in to collect the money from the "leader" and, if he didn't have it, he would be taken away and he wouldn't come back. The next day, there would be a new "leader" in his place. Sometimes the kids would be made to do different things for the dealers. Girls would have to have sex with them and the gangs would use them to run guns as well as drugs. The girls would give birth on the streets in public and the children were all mixed up. Nobody knew who their real father was. Brother and sister would get older and pair up, having more children – *together*.

Unintentional incest.

These things I learned through observation as the days went by. I discovered that most of the kids were born in Cracolândia and didn't know any different. But some had just got into drugs and their families had thrown them out so they, like me, had nowhere else to go.

The dealers would get people deliberately hooked on crack by offering them the first hit or two for free. They knew once the kids took a fix, they wouldn't be able to wait for the next one. There was nothing else in their lives – no love, no prospects, nothing else to live for – so the crack became their lover, their family, their only friend.

Once you entered Cracolândia, it was a miracle if you came back out. I often pretended to smoke the pipe to keep the pushers off my back. The mortality rate was high and life expectancy in the gangs was no longer than eighteen – the age of Luiz, who was the oldest in our group.

I went into the city centre to pickpocket and hustle every day and every evening when I came back, somebody I knew would be gone. They had either been stabbed or shot or set alight or taken by the police. Or abducted by some pervert looking for prey and coming down to take a girl – or a boy.

The street kids were constantly motivated by fear and nobody ever said anything or complained to the police, because corruption was so rife. Nobody knew anything about human rights, they just believed that *this* was life. Survival and self-preservation are the greatest of all human instincts and people have no conscience about what they need to do to stay alive. So they folded their fear into their next fix and allowed the illusion of their lives to possess them.

The little group I hung out with taught me how to survive on the streets. The basic rules were:

17

1. If a drug dealer tells you to do something, do it.

2. If you see the police, run.

3. When you sleep, do it with one eye open.

It was largely accepted that the worst thing was to be taken away by the police because it meant either torture or death, or both. Either way, you were never seen again.

We would beg and steal in the city centre and pretend to have wounds on our bodies by placing a cut of rancid meat from a bin and covering it with a rag. We'd leave the meat showing to make our "wound" look infected.

Other times we'd collect rubbish from the tips of São Paulo – cans, cardboard, metal and old furniture to recycle for cash. We would collect it in two-wheeled trolleys and sometimes it could weigh as much as a hundred kilos. We'd push and pull the trolleys a long way to the recycling depot and they'd give us a few *reais* for it, but it took a lot of effort and expended a lot of energy for very little reward.

Some of the kids were intimidated into becoming informants for the police. They didn't last long. Others would watch for rival gangs and warn the drug dealers when strangers approached.

The real tragedy was that they honestly believed this was all life had to offer people like them. This was their lot and so they lived for the day. They had no dreams, no future, no fixed place in space and time, so the only thing that motivated them was their next hit – their window in the wall. They longed to look through it again, if only for a brief moment. They were hopelessly addicted to their addiction, and that longing of the soul was their only raison d'être.

Every now and then the *Cardecista* Catholics would turn up with food and clothing and pretend to talk to us like we were human beings. But they, too, wanted something.

They would bring their bibles and preach, trying to get us to go to church. They would come in big groups to offer themselves some degree of protection, never in ones or twos. The people in Cracolândia all believed in God and prayed that God would help them.

He never did.

I would hear them at night, begging Him for a better life, surrounded by the darkness. But God didn't hear them. He only listened to the proud and the pretentious, and what good was giving people a little bit of food and a blanket a couple of times a month?

The preachers weren't really doing anything for the street kids, just offering something to alleviate their own guilty consciences for colluding with the corruption. Some charities handed out utensils and other basic things for people to cook and clean with, but you wouldn't have them for long if you didn't carry them about with you, and that was practically impossible.

Despite the poverty and hardship, and the intense level of addiction, I was always amazed by the generosity of people who had absolutely nothing to give. After seeing the lives these street kids had to endure, I decided I had no right to be depressed. I was going to fight the demon that had haunted me for so long and *never* let it take control of me again, as it had so often in the past.

CHAPTER TWO
LAGEADO

I was born Rozana Ramos in February 1973, in the small village of Lageado in southern Brazil.

Lageado wasn't exactly a village back then, more like a cluster of shacks on farmland that was close to the big house of the landowner. We didn't have the things you would expect of a village. There were no streets, shops, bicycles or kindly eccentric characters, just planted fields surrounded by scrubland and forest.

The landowner kept animals on the farmland where I lived – pigs, cattle, horses, chickens and geese. He also had a big plantation in the *Vespeira* area, which was two hours away, where he grew rice, corn, tea and tobacco.

I was the third youngest of ten children, two of whom had died before I was born – a boy from meningitis and a baby girl from some kind of fever. Nobody knew the exact cause. There were no hospitals or doctors to treat them, so they just died.

My earliest recollections are from when I was about four-years-old, crying because my mother had gone to work on the plantation and left me. It's strange and elusive how some far off things never fade from memory, yet many more recent events disappear quickly, like evaporating mist above a forest canopy.

Even now, when I close my eyes all these long years later, I sometimes feel as though I'm back there, standing under the *palmeira* trees and feeling the heat of the sun on my face. Memories are real things. They can be seen and touched and felt, like diamonds or pain. They remind us of who we once were; who we will never be again.

My older brothers and sisters all worked as domestic servants and only came home when they lost a job and were looking for another. All except my eldest brother, Antonio. He was a violent drunk and he stayed at home. I lived with my mother, father, younger brother and sister, and Antonio, in a hut that my parents built themselves from wood they chopped and hauled from the forest.

Rain came through the roof and it had no floor, just hard-packed soil. We only had four beds and when my older siblings were home between jobs, it was incredibly crowded. My father slept on a cot and I slept with my mother and younger brother and sister. The rest of them shared the other two beds, with girls in one and boys in the other. The beds were wooden and also built by my parents. We lay on mattresses made from fertilizer sacks filled with straw. There was a brick fireplace for cooking and a bench for sitting.

Nothing else.

We had no running water or electricity in our village and the only means of transport was by horse and cart. My parents both had to work on the plantation from 5:30am to 7:00pm for subsistence wages. My mother also washed the clothes of the landowner's family for no pay, just to get the materials for the homemade soap she used. It was made from pigs' guts that were mixed with ash and soda crystals and boiled up, then left to solidify. She used this to wash our clothes in a stream.

After work she would sometimes go hunting to try and catch a rabbit or a small deer or some other animal for dinner. She also had to fetch firewood to cook with and she was always much more of a provider than my father.

My father would only work in my mother's company – he didn't like to work alone. Work only had meaning for him if she was there. Sometimes she would be annoyed with him because he would fall into a daydream and, without her supervision, the chores would not get completed.

He was a very laid back man with idle dreams inside his head, but I loved him very much, almost as much as my mother.

Life had made my mother hard, the complete opposite of my father. He was light-hearted and felt things inside his soul. Maybe my mother did too, but she never showed it. My father liked to laugh and dance with me and he told me stories that came from another world, far away from Lageado. Sometimes work intruded on that place he went to, inside himself, and he would try to ignore it and ramble with his dreams. But he had to work when he was with my mother and, when my parents went to the plantation in the morning, us three youngest children were left alone every day to fend for ourselves.

The first thing we had to do each day was walk a mile to fetch drinking water from the stream down the valley. The water was fresh in the summer, but come winter it was frozen and we'd have to break the ice to get to it. Once we did, it would still be warm underneath. But the stream was always full of frogs – I had a phobia about them and still don't like them to this day. We had to carry the water back up the hill in buckets, spilling it over fallen trees until we reached our hut.

Next we would decide how to feed ourselves, because there was never anything to eat in the hut. There were two places we could go. The first was Mrs Izabel's. Mrs Izabel was the landowner's wife. She had a family of four boys and four girls who lived in the big house not too far from our hut. She frowned a lot and spoke very little in a quiet voice. She would only take one of us in to eat at a time, so we took it in turns and the other two would have to wait. If my brother was taken in for breakfast, usually bread and home-made jam, I could go in for lunch of pork and beans, and my sister could ask for the leftovers in the afternoon. Some days Mrs Izabel would be in a melancholy mood, trying to cope with her own children, and would tell us to go somewhere else for food.

If that happened, her son Ramon, who was just a few months older than me, would secretly bring food from the house when he was able to. He was a beautiful person and I was in love with him, even though I didn't know what love was at the time.

He wore nice clothes, his hair was properly cut and his skin was so soft. My clothes were ragged hand-me-downs, I cut my own hair and my skin was rough from being out in the weather. I had nits on my head and rashes on my skin. Worms that distended my belly would emerge from different orifices of my body and I was always filthy dirty. Still, as time went by, a close friendship formed between Ramon and me. It was something really special, more than mere friendship. There's a closeness that children have, whether they're rich or poor, clean or dirty; that connection of childhood before prides and prejudices are learned from adults.

It wasn't like he felt sorry for me or that I felt reverence for him. It was just a gentle affection for each other that two very young people experienced, in a place that offered little else to disrupt our harmony.

If Mrs Izabel was too heavy hearted and Ramon couldn't smuggle something out, the second place we would go was Rosemary's house. Rosemary was Mrs Izabel's eldest daughter and she married a man the family didn't approve of. She had her own house on the land and her own three children, and in many ways was the complete opposite of her mother. She liked to talk a lot, her voice was bright and bosomy, and she always had a smile on her face. She was one of the kindest people I've ever met and she would always give us any beans, rice or bread she could spare. The problem was, she rarely had enough to feed her own family.

If these two food sources failed, we would have to either beg in the street or steal from farmers, taking their grapes or watermelons or sweetcorn. If we begged, it would be in a marketplace of sorts that was some distance away. One small shop sold food and alcohol to the farmers who gathered to barter.

We were never welcome there and were treated like outcasts; inferior little gypsies, and they would chase us away. If we stole, we had to be stealthy like animals, because if the farmers caught us, they would beat us badly. There was a small primary school in the area and sometimes we'd break in and steal whatever food had been discarded by the teacher or the children who could afford to go there; food that was surplus to their requirements.

Ramon had an elder brother called Daniel who was about six or seven years older than me. In contrast to Ramon, he was a cruel, sadistic boy and he made my young life a misery.

'Hey, Rozana!'

'What?'

'Suck my toe.'

'No!'

'I'll give you some money.'

When you need food, it's remarkable what you'll do.

So I sucked his toe and he laughed at me for being a fool and believing he would pay me for doing such a thing. I think Ramon's family didn't like the idea of him being so close to a *negrinha* girl like me, who had nits, skin rashes and worms and was filthy all the time. Mrs Izabel would do anything to prevent him from playing with me. She stopped taking me into the house for food and made me eat it elsewhere. Daniel's bullying might have been meant as a warning for me to keep my distance from his brother.

Unfortunately, things got worse and Daniel decided to take his abuse to another level. He began to sexually violate me by making me take off all my clothes, which was hugely embarrassing to a six-year-old like me. Then he did things to me that weren't right. We both knew they weren't right, but he did them anyway. If I refused to do what he wanted, he threatened to beat me and to tell his mother not to feed me anymore. He said his father would throw my parents off the land and we'd have nowhere to live.

I felt contaminated inside and was sure I'd slowly rot away. Eventually, these sins would show themselves on the outside; on my face and my body, and everyone would know how bad I'd been.

I would go to hell and remain there forever.

Daniel hung round with three or four boys his own age and they all bullied me. They would form a circle around me and throw snakes, or push me from one to the other, or smear me with the blood from dead birds and animals. It developed into a daily routine that I was unable to stop and my life became a living nightmare.

I was an ignorant girl back then and so I didn't know any better. I believed this treatment was normal and a part of my life, a punishment for being so poor. So I just accepted it. Nobody cared. It was what happened to bad girls like me.

Ramon found out about his brother's bullying and tried to stop it, but he was only six, like me, and Daniel didn't take much notice of him. My own older brother, Antonio, was too drunk all the time to know what was going on and my parents were always working. Even if they knew, there wasn't much they could do. Like me, they would fear losing their jobs and being thrown out of the hut, so I accepted the abuse for everyone's sake.

When I was young, rumour and superstition played a big part in the lives of the rural people of Lageado. They told stories about ghosts and demons and escaped murderers. Lies were circulating that many people who left for work in the morning never returned home because they were killed or abducted by some monster or maniac.

I believed these tales and was in constant fear that every time my mother went off to work, she would never come back – ever. I would pine for her and when she *did* come home, I'd be so glad to see her. The relief was so strong I forgot about whatever happened to me that day and I'd believe tomorrow would be better.

We were Catholic and there was a small church that had no priest. Ramon's father said the Mass every Sunday and the priest would only come if he was paid. Then he would turn up in a big Jeep to collect his money and give us his expensive blessing and say some words about the rewards we could expect in the next life, while he enjoyed them right now.

My mother made me a yellow dress from someone's hand-me-down to wear to the church on Sundays. I liked to look nice in it. Maybe it's why Daniel abused me so badly. Maybe it was the yellow dress he was taking his frustration out on, and not me at all. *It was the dress's fault.*

There would always be a party at Christmas time and *Papai Noel* would come and give out presents to the rich children. I always wondered why he liked them but didn't like us poor kids. I only realised later that the presents were paid for by their parents and our parents couldn't afford any for us.

Time passed so slowly in that far off life. Weeks felt like months, days felt like weeks, hours like felt days and minutes felt like hours. Everything was moving in slow motion – to me, at least. But time was inanimate, so it couldn't move. It was I, by my choices, who was moving within my own limited concept of what time ought to be. In reality, everything was transient and nothing could be depended on to remain the same. Nor did I want it to.

The village considered me to be precocious, a schemer, the cleverest of the younger children in the area. The organiser of mischief. My parents would be gone from early in the morning, before dawn, and I would be left in charge of my younger brother and sister.

Once, I found a pair of scissors and decided to practice being a hairdresser. I cut my sister's hair down to her scalp and I shaved her eyebrows with my father's razor. Other young children came round to watch as I displayed my talents outside our little hut and it was so much fun I decided to style their hair and eyebrows too. I thought they all looked amazing and so did they, until their parents saw what I'd done. They came after me, chased me around and finally caught me. They held me down and shaved off all my hair and eyebrows, warning me they'd shave off my skin if I did anything like that again.

So I retired from the hairdressing trade.

By the time I turned seven, my friendship with Ramon was unbreakable, no matter what his family or his brother tried to do about it. We hung out together all the time. Some days we would go swimming in the man-made *represa* that was part of the stream from which we drew water. Other times we'd sneak up to the loft in his house and look through old pictures. Most days we would dig for the treasure we believed was buried on his father's land.

It was rumoured that Ramon's great-grandmother, Buena, had buried a pot of gold there and it remained undiscovered for hundreds of years. If you tried to find it at night, she would appear in a flowing dress and long black hair to take you away to hell.

We always searched for it during the day.

Eventually we would get tired and sit under a tree to make plans for the future. *When* we found the treasure, we'd leave Lageado to get married, buy a cow and live happily ever after.

But Ramon was due to start at the primary school and we wouldn't be able to see each other so often after that. He'd be studying so would have little time to wander about and daydream. I wouldn't be going to school because we couldn't afford to pay for materials like books, pencils and all the other items I'd need to learn with.

We couldn't bear the thought of being separated like that. We decided it would be better if we both died. At least then we'd be together. We thought about it for a long time, but couldn't find a way to kill ourselves that wasn't painful, so we decided to run away together instead.

The next morning, we met behind the old tea factory. It was only used for three to four months throughout the year during the tea-processing season. The rest of the time it was used as a playground by the children. Ramon had a bag of clothes and I had nothing, because I had no other clothes except the ones on my back. Apart

27

from the yellow dress, and that dress would be seen from far away, so it couldn't come with us. It would have to stay and Daniel would have to find another dress to molest.

We set off across the fields and into the scrubland and forest. Ramon sang a song while we walked, one he'd written especially for me. It was called *Together We Are Beautiful*.

♪ *You walked into my life*
And now it's like a party
A party only for you
No other people invited
And it's beautiful
Yes it's beautiful ♪

After about an hour or so of walking, we came across a huge cherry tree in full fruit. There was a spring with clear running water not far away and it seemed like the ideal place to spend the rest of our lives together. We'd never be hungry or thirsty and we'd always have each other.

We climbed the tree and stayed there, talking and laughing and eating wild cherries until the sun began to fade from the sky. Then we climbed back down, gathered up a bed of leaves and lay together until we fell asleep.

The next thing we knew, someone was kicking us awake. We opened our eyes to see Daniel and some of his friends standing over us. They beat me and kicked me and dragged Ramon away, leaving me bloody and bruised on our childbed of leaves.

I never saw Ramon alive again.

CHAPTER THREE
SCHOOL

My brother Antonio was different from the rest of us. He became very violent when he was drunk, and he was always drunk. I think it was because of what happened when he was seven-years-old and my oldest brother, Joseph, was eight – before I was born.

Joseph had his own plot of corn and everyone said he would own a farm one day and be a man of integrity and vision. The oldest son, leading his family forward through the parted seas of serfdom, away from poverty. But then he got meningitis and became very sick.

He would say to my mother, over and over, ". . . don't let me die. Don't let me die," but without a doctor, there was nothing she could do.

Antonio saw all of this.

He also went with my mother when she tried to carry Joseph to another village where they had a pharmacy. It was a four-day walk and they stopped to rest in a derelict hut one night. Joseph was very weak and he turned and spoke to my mother.

'Don't carry me anymore.'

'Why not?'

'It's the end for me.'

'No . . .'

'It's alright. I know where I'm going. It's a better place.'

He died before he got to harvest his plot of corn.

They carried his body back to Lageado and my father made a coffin so he could be buried in the local graveyard.

Antonio started drinking after that, even though he was very young. He had become the oldest sibling and the burden of expectation fell upon him. Perhaps he couldn't accept that tragic legacy, or maybe it was the trauma of seeing his brother die like that.

He mostly drank *cachaça*, a cheap white rum containing 70% alcohol. He would drink two bottles a day when he could afford it. Then he would come home, throw things about, beat everyone up and even kill cats and dogs if they got in his way. He once chopped the head off a little pet dog I had and I cried for days.

My father, being a peaceful, gentle man who hated confrontation, would go to bed with his idle dreams and pretend to be asleep so he didn't have to confront the helpless anger – in case his own helpless anger surfaced in sympathy. For all of his strengths, he wasn't good at accepting responsibility as head of a family. He left that to my mother.

Antonio would cry like a baby the next morning and say he was sorry for the things he did – until he did them again.

After a week without seeing Ramon, I couldn't stand it any longer. I had to go to his house and see how he was. It had been the longest week of my life. I waited for him every morning under a *palmiera* tree, the same tree I waited under every evening for my mother, but he didn't come. I was afraid to go to the big house in case Daniel beat me up again, but I was so worried about Ramon.

I wondered if his parents had sent him away somewhere. I knew he had an uncle in Porto Alegre and maybe they'd sent him there to get him away from me. Maybe he would never be allowed to come back, at least until we were too old to find the treasure and get married and buy a cow and live happily ever after.

The thought made me cry. We should have died instead of running away. We should have been braver; stronger.

Finally, after a week of waiting, I decided I had to go to the house, even if it did mean risking another beating. When I got there, I saw a lot of unusual activity outside. Cars were pulling up and people were entering the home. I stayed some distance away and waited, hoping Ramon would come out and I could wave him towards me.

I waited for a long time, but there was no sign of him.

So many people came and went that I assumed there was some kind of occasion – maybe a birthday or an anniversary. Then Daniel appeared at the door. I moved behind a tree in case he saw me. I watched him for a while and noticed that he looked sad. His head hung down and he stared at the ground. It took me a while to realise he was crying and so, cautiously, I decided to approach him.

'Daniel . . .'

He didn't answer. He didn't even seem to notice me.

'Why are you crying?'

When he looked at me, it was as if he didn't see me; as if he was looking through me. His voice was hoarse when he finally spoke.

'It's Ramon . . .'

'What about Ramon?'

'He's dead.'

It took a moment to register and I thought I misheard him – that he'd said "his head" or "he's fled," or something like that. Slowly, though, the words sank in. He was telling me Ramon had died. I screamed and sank to my knees. Daniel just turned and walked back into the house, but I stayed on the ground, sobbing, feeling a pain inside like a piranha was eating my heart. If Ramon was dead, I would have to die too. But first I had to see him, in case Daniel was playing a cruel trick on me.

I got to my feet and followed a group of strangers in through the front door. I tried to make myself invisible so his family wouldn't see me and throw me back out. I followed the flow of visitors to a room and saw Ramon lying on a bed. He was dressed in a blue shirt, but the rest of his body was covered up.

He looked different. Older. More grown up. Not the young boy who had run away with me and climbed the cherry tree. His eyes were closed and there was a kind of half smile on his face. He didn't look dead, more like he was pretending. I wanted to go over and shake him; to tell him to get up because he was upsetting me.

His family were all there and people kept coming and going all the time, paying their respects. Everyone was too devastated to notice me. I got pushed around and found myself in another room with a long wooden table. The table was laden with food and everybody was helping themselves to bread and meat, but for the first time in my life, I wasn't hungry. Any other time, it would have been like Christmas and I'd have gorged myself until I threw up, but at that moment the food meant nothing to me. It was revolting, and it was equally revolting to see people stuffing it into their mouths without caring. Just then, some men came through carrying a long white box. They went into the room where Ramon was lying and I watched from the open doorway as they placed him inside.

He didn't wake up as I'd hoped.

He was really dead.

I hid under the table and cried.

Outside, the men had made a fire and drank *quentão*, which is made with wine and cloves, to keep themselves warm. I was thinking about how I would kill myself and follow Ramon to heaven. There was a plant called *erva-moura* that grew in the vicinity of Lageado which was said to be poisonous and my mother always warned me not to eat it, so I went to a place where it was growing and ate its green berries. It didn't kill me. It just caused severe stomach pain and made me vomit for several days.

Sadly, I recovered.

By the time I got better, Ramon was already buried. I visited his grave and knelt beside it to say a prayer for him, *"Pai Nosso, que estais nos Céus . . ."*

They told me how he died. He was going with his family to attend a relative's funeral in another village. Ramon was riding on top of the truck and wanted to be with his mother at the front. As he tried to climb down, he fell and the back wheels of the truck went over him.

After that, I lost track of time and just wandered around aimlessly. There was no hope of a better life any more. All the simple plans I'd made with Ramon would never come true. I didn't have the courage to kill myself and I knew, if I tried, I would only fail again. However, I realised there was no need to, for I still possessed Ramon in my memory. The remembrance of our love and friendship was mine alone. To keep. No one could take it away from me. Ever.

That's when I decided to go away. I had to leave Lageado.

It was very common for poor children to work for richer families, to help their parents make ends meet or just work for food. The next farm to the one owned by Ramon's family was called *Fazenda dos Alemão* and was owned by Germans. It was a big soya plantation and they kept milking cows as well. I heard the lady was looking for a girl to take care of her baby, so I walked the five miles to the *Fazenda* and asked for the job.

'How old are you?'

'Nine.'

I lied.

'And you have experience?'

'I have looked after my younger sister and brother since they were born.'

The land was shared by different members of the family, whose name was Wisiniter. They were Protestant and had their own church, with all the houses in walking distance of each other. It was like a little settlement and they communicated with me in Portuguese because I couldn't speak German.

The lady who hired me was called Herta and the job was very easy. All I needed to do was sit by the baby and call her if he cried.

German people had different values to Brazilians and Herta was dismayed when she found out I'd never been to school. It was soon arranged that she would pay for the books, pencils and paper I needed and I would go to school in the mornings before looking after the baby in the afternoons and evenings.

A few weeks later, I started in year one of the local primary. It was strange. Ramon was the one who was supposed to be attending school, and now he never would. Instead, purely by chance, I was being educated.

The school was an old wooden building with a little kitchen and a wooden floor that us children had to wash after lessons. There was one classroom with a blackboard and not enough desks for the dozen or so pupils that went there.

The teacher's name was Angela and she came from outside to teach us. Sometimes she slept in the kitchen. During winter, it became too cold for poor kids like myself to hold our pencils because we had no gloves, so Angela would send us out into the sun to warm our hands. Just like my father, I would spend this time daydreaming in the golden glow, trying to think about all the things that must be out there in the world. I wanted to know everything. I wanted to drink from the Pierian spring of knowledge that had been denied to me until my education began, and my thoughts flew up into the air and stayed there, like silver moths.

I liked school and I was a quick and eager learner. Life was good with the Wisiniter family while it lasted. I had three meals a day and as much milk as I could drink.

Herta was a very kind and pretty woman who treated me like I was part of the family. In the evenings when she went to milk the cows, I would put Junior in his basket and go down to the barn to watch her working. Sometimes she'd let me have a go. We'd laugh and drink big glasses of milk fresh from the cow. She bought ointment to get rid of my rashes and picked the nits from my hair, but she couldn't do anything for the worms that distended my stomach and wriggled out, sometimes through my nose.

On Sundays I would go to church with the family. I liked the Protestant faith better than Catholicism. It was friendlier and more easy going, with singing and no threats of eternal damnation for girls like me, who allowed older boys to sexually abuse them.

I would also play with the German children in the family and we'd do each other's hair. Herta made me a green dress out of some rough hessian material, but I didn't like it because it was too tight and my distended belly made me look like I was pregnant. She also gave me a pair of flip-flops and it was the first time I'd ever worn anything on my feet. They felt strange and it took me a while to get used to them. It was like I had walked in something that was stuck to the soles of my feet and I wanted to scrape it off.

All-in-all, things were good, but after a few months went by I began to have vivid nightmares that my mother had either died or been killed. Despite my father's storytelling, she was the person I loved most in the world and I missed her terribly. I was still just a child and I felt guilty for being so happy – guilty about the food I was eating when the rest of my family had nothing. It's hard to believe that I would want to go back to the dirt and hunger and violence of Lageado when I was so happy at *Fazenda dos Alemão*, but I did. I wanted to go back to my mother.

Herta was upset when I told her. She'd invested time in me and had plans for my future. She tried to persuade me to stay, but I couldn't. Something deeper than the happiness I'd experienced was pulling me back, that sybaritic thing which is ingrained in all of us, coded into our DNA, into our creatureness. Our blood.

Herta gave me two bottles of milk and some coffee for my mother and wished me luck. Then I left to walk the five miles home.

I was eight-years-old when I returned home and for the first few days it was nice to be back. I was glad to see my mother, younger brother and sister again, as well as the familiar surroundings of Lageado.

I was still going to school because I had the materials Herta bought for me and that gave me great status with the poor kids – *prestige* – that turned me into a little celebrity. Everyone wanted to know all about what I'd learned, about reading and arithmetic. They wanted to know what it was like to drink milk every day, to have a shower, to use a toilet, not to be hungry.

It was a strange thing but I felt special, different somehow, like I wasn't one of *them* anymore. I'd had an experience no one else had had and it changed me, even if I didn't know it. I spent hours playing and swimming with my brother and sister and Rosemary's children. I told them lots of stories – some were true and others made up to help enhance my new status.

But I was worried about meeting Daniel in my green dress, the one that made me look pregnant. Maybe he liked green more than yellow. Maybe he envied green more than yellow. Maybe he would want to hurt green more than he wanted to hurt yellow. I hadn't seen him since that day he was crying outside his house. What if he'd told someone what we did – that I'd allowed him to do those things to me?

As a child, the worst thing wasn't the physical pain of abuse – it was the shame. It was *my* fault. If I wasn't bad, it wouldn't have happened. I lived with the constant worry of being found out, because I believed everyone would blame me.

I did see Daniel again, but it was from a distance. He seemed distracted and didn't bother with me. Maybe he was afraid to, because anyone who'd spent time with the Germans was respected.

Or maybe he just didn't like green.

Our hut was small and dirty and everyone smoked, even my younger sister. They smoked the rough unrefined tobacco that grew on the *Vespeira* plantation and they rolled it in the skins of the corn. We didn't have a bathroom and had to wash in the stream. All this seemed perfectly normal before I went to *Fazenda dos Alemão*, but now that I'd seen something better, I didn't want to have to live that kind of life any more.

The novelty of being back home soon wore off.

During the time I was living in Herta's house, I felt guilty for being so happy. But I came to believe it was the kind of life I was entitled to – waking up each morning and not having to fight over a crust of bread, having a sweater to put on when it was cold and having a shower before bed.

As time went by, the school required me to have more and more things my mother couldn't afford – more paper and pencils and books. I was told I would have to leave, but I didn't want to. I was so happy there. It didn't seem fair to have to give it up as I was doing so well. However, it got to the point where I didn't even have a pencil to write with and the other schoolchildren were making fun of me.

So I left.

Then I met a family who was looking for a girl to help with housework. It was at the yearly Catholic church party. Somebody told them I was a good worker and they offered me the job. Their names were Sanata and Silvio Müller and they were Brazilian with German origins. They told me their daughter was a teacher and that I would be able to go back to school. It seemed perfect to me. They promised to come and collect me the following weekend and I was really excited. I was going to live in a lovely big house, have as much food as I could eat and be able to go back to school. It was a dream come true.

The days dragged past and I couldn't sleep the night before they were due to arrive. It was a Sunday and I went down to the stream early to clean my teeth and wash myself with our homemade soap. It stank, but it got things clean and I was very keen to make a good impression. My mother was more worried than the first time I left because I was going further away, but she didn't try to stop me.

'The best thing I can do is let you go, Rozana. But don't forget . . .'

'What, *mãe*?'

'What feeds one dog, feeds ten.'

She meant I could always come back if things didn't work out.

The Müllers turned up on Sunday evening in a big car to take me away. I was so happy to be leaving Lageado again. I even wore my yellow church dress and the flip-flops Herta Wisiniter had given me. I also carried a small plastic bag that contained my few other clothes – all except the green dress. I left it behind because I was tired of looking pregnant. And it would still be there if I ever came back – to keep Daniel at bay.

I waved to my mother and left, for the second time, to find a better life.

After a short half an hour drive I could see the big house in the distance. It was a mansion. I felt so lucky leaving that poor, hungry place and moving into a palace. There was a large gate and a driveway up to the *casa grande*, which was painted blue with a big balcony all round it.

I followed the Müllers into a large room with a long glass table and a beautiful shiny wooden floor. Coloured candles glowed on side shelves and wonderful paintings of people and landscapes hung from the walls, as well as a clock with a little bird that came out and said "cuckoo." Soft, fluffy rugs were scattered around the house and it was like walking on clouds when I stepped on them. It seemed like a *conto de fadas* to me and I couldn't believe this place actually existed. I was an excited child and I wanted to run and explore my new world, but a stern voice shouted at me.

'Stop!'

And so began my years of slavery.

CHAPTER FOUR
SLAVERY

I was taken to the loft at the top of the frowning house, up a very steep and narrow flight of steps. My room was tiny and looked like it hadn't been used for a long time. There was a sloping roof and bare dusty floorboards and a small wooden bed with a thin foam mattress. A small stool and some artificial flowers were placed in a vase in a corner of the room and dark cobwebs hung from the ceiling. I was frightened to have to stay there alone, as I'd never slept alone before. We always shared the beds at home, and even at the Wisiniters, I shared a bed with Junior.

All through the previous week I'd imagined having a room fit for a princess, even though I had absolutely no idea what a princess's room would look like. Still, I expected something better than what confronted me. I expected a degree of luxury and some laughter and light. Everything about my new room was dark and dismal. The steep stairs that I found so difficult to climb were creepy, the cobwebs were creepy, the artificial flowers were creepy. How could I escape if something or someone came after me up in this devil-trap?

It took me a long time to get to sleep that night. I kept remembering the words the Müllers said to me as I made my way up the steep wooden steps.

'You'll see the house tomorrow, when you are cleaning it.'

The artificial flowers cast grotesque shadows in the moonlight that came through my bare window. The plastic stems and petals looked like the legs and bodies of giant spiders and they seemed to be getting closer to my bed. They weren't flowers any more, they were fiends.

I tried to pray – *Ave Maria, cheia de graçe, o Senhor é convosco* – but I couldn't focus my mind on the words. I was surrounded by an undulating sea of anxiety and my bed was a shrinking island, getting smaller by the moment. I eventually fell asleep through sheer exhaustion, but what seemed like only five minutes later, I heard my name being called loudly.

'Rozana!'

I climbed out of the thin bed and went to the door. It was Silvio, summoning me from downstairs.

'Get up Rozana!'

I got dressed and made my way down to the kitchen, trying not to stumble and fall down the narrow steps. It was 5:30am. I was so tired I just wanted to go back to sleep. He told me to light the fire, but there was no thin kindling like I used at home. He told me to pour some kind of accelerant, maybe petrol, on the wood and then stand back and throw a lighted match to set it ablaze. I felt this was too dangerous and didn't want to do it, which irritated him greatly. He snatched the matches from my hand and did it himself, but said I would have to do it from then on.

After that, I had to go outside and feed the animals. The Müllers had a farm at the back of their mansion. It was a big plot of land and they kept about thirty pigs, six cows and a hundred chickens. They also had a lot of goats that roamed wild across the land. I had to get the corn and other animal feed from a barn and distribute it among the livestock. It was tiring work and I'd still not had anything to eat.

It was almost 9:00am when I got back to the house. Sanata and her daughter Cleo, who was nineteen and studying to be a teacher, were up by then and had prepared breakfast of coffee, ham, fried eggs and homemade bread. I was starving and approached the table, but Silvio pushed me away.

'You do not eat with us!'

He told me I hadn't yet watered the pigs and I should go do

it now. The water came from a well and had to be drawn up by hand in a bucket. I was still only eight-years-old and this was a very difficult task that took me a long time. Still, I kept going, thinking about the breakfast that would be waiting for me when I finished.

By the time I got back, the table had been cleared and all that was left was a cup of black coffee and half a slice of bread. I sat on the stairs and cried. Tears rolled down my face and dripped from my chin into the coffee. To think I had left home again for this.

Cleo came and asked why I was weeping. I didn't want to tell her the truth, that I was disappointed and disillusioned. She might have called me ungrateful and threw me out onto the remote road. I wouldn't know how to get home and would be eaten by a wild animal or mutilated by an escaped murderer.

'I miss my mother.'

'You've only been here one day, Rozana.'

That made me cry even more, thinking about all the days that stretched ahead.

'Shut up! Don't be such a *bebê*.'

It wasn't long before Silvio and Sanata came to find out what the commotion was. All three of them were shouting at me, telling me to shut up. Then someone slapped me across the face, but I can't remember who. They dragged me out onto the balcony by my hair and left me there, like a frightened dog. I cried so much I felt sick and would have thrown up, had there been anything in my stomach. Later, Cleo came back out.

'Come with me.'

'Where?'

'I'll show you how to clean the house.'

I followed and she explained what my work would be. As well as feeding and watering the animals twice a day, I would have to clean the whole house, wash up, weed the orchard, bring in firewood and water the plants in the vegetable garden.

By the time I was finished, I was completely exhausted. They

41

had dinner at 8:00pm and, again, I was not allowed near the table. I was given a plate of black beans and rice and I had to eat it on the balcony. After dinner, I had to do the washing up, which I finished about 9:30pm. Then I went to bed and fell into an uneasy and fretful sleep. That was the first day of my new life over with.

I was awoken at 5:30am again the following morning and my body ached bone deep from working the previous day. That second day was very much the same and during the many days that followed, the Müllers increased my workload. I was expected to clean out the cow stables and the pig sties and help with the milking and collect eggs from the chickens.

I cried for the whole of that first week – I was miserable, tired and hungry, and I missed my mother so much. I thought I'd have a day off on the weekend but by then Silvio had given me an alarm clock and told me to set it for 5:30am every morning so he didn't have to get up to wake me. Worse still, he didn't work on the weekends, so I had to do everything without his help. This meant the days I thought I was going to rest actually became the days when I had to work the hardest. They also began feeding me leftovers, like they did with their pigs. They would scrape the food onto a plate and it would all get mixed in together – jelly and beans and cake and rice.

Because I was so busy all the time, the hours and days went quickly and I was beginning to get used to the heavy routine. Before I came to the Müllers, it was arranged that I could go home every other weekend for a day, from Saturday afternoon to Sunday afternoon. On the second week, the thought of seeing my mother filled me with joy. Saturday came and, for the first time, I jumped rather than crawled out of bed. I was so excited. I completed the list of chores they'd given me quickly so I'd be ready when my father came. When Silvio got up, he was angry rather than pleased that I'd done the work so soon.

'Why did it take you twice as long to do the same jobs yesterday?'
'I don't know. . . '

42

'Little *preguiçosa molenga*!'

I thought he was going to beat me or leave me without food, but instead he said I couldn't go home to see my family. It would be another two weeks before I could visit. They could have cut my fingers off and it wouldn't have hurt so much.

My father arrived in the afternoon to pick me up. He looked fragile and tired, having walked a long way in the heat of the day. I could see him through the window and I wanted to run out to him, but they kept me inside the house and Sanata went to the door.

'Rozana's not well.'

'Oh . . . what's wrong with her?'

'Nothing too serious, but she won't be able to walk all that way.'

My father just smiled obligingly in that easy-going way of his, turned and walked away. I could see him going, trudging down the driveway and I wanted to shout out after him, to call him back and tell him I was alright and perfectly able to walk all the way home. Silvio held a firm hand over my mouth and I could not.

The weeks melted into months, flowing into each other and becoming one big blur. I wondered why I had to be born as me, Rozana Ramos. Why could I not have been someone else – a rich girl, or a girl from another country where children didn't have to work, or a prodigy who could play the piano? Even then, I felt there was more to life. I felt there was some kind of destiny, a future that was linked to the bigger horizon. I continued to work a lot and eat very little and I missed my mother more and more. Whenever it was time for me to go home for a visit, they found a reason not to let me go.

Molenga became my nickname, which meant something like shirker in English. The shadows of the artificial flowers at night became more oppressive. I began having nightmares and I would wake up to the ghosts lowering over me, threatening me, staring down at me and saying: "You will never leave here. Ha ha ha!"

The lack of food and sleep made me ill, but I had to carry on working, no matter how I felt. Whenever they all went out and I was left alone in the house I cowered in a corner and did nothing – because I was always afraid something bad was hiding in one of the rooms and it would jump out and devour me. I was never used to being alone and I hated it. I even preferred the company of the cruel Müllers to being on my own in that sinister and surly house.

The months turned into a year and Cleo made me a cake for my ninth birthday. It was one of the few kindnesses I received there, but it was short-lived and I was soon back in their bad books for one thing or another. Eventually, it came to the point when I couldn't take it any longer, I'd gone far beyond my limit of endurance. So one day, when they all went out, I packed my bag and left.

It was a long way home and I didn't really know the way. I was still afraid of being mauled or murdered, but I just had to get away. Staying was far worse than going. I wasn't far down the road when I was caught by a policeman from a nearby village who just so happened to be going out with Cleo. He dragged me back and told me if I ran away again, he would put me and my whole family in jail for life. He also said that if I told anyone about the conversation, he would shoot me in the feet, so I'd never be able to walk again.

From then on, my life became worse than ever.

It was always a struggle to pull the water bucket up from the well, and once, when I was really tired and not feeling at all good, it felt much heavier than usual and I let the handle slip. It spun round so fast and hit me on the head, just over my eye. I was thrown backwards onto the ground and when I managed to get up again, I was cut so badly that the bone above my right eyebrow was exposed and I was covered in blood. I didn't scream or cry, I just felt relieved because I thought they would let me rest. However, when I went to tell them about the accident, they just got angry.

'You are useless, *Molenga*!'

Silvio got to his feet.

'I'll draw the water for the pigs. You go cut the grass.'

44

They didn't get a doctor or dress the wound with a bandage or anything. It was very sore and the bone was exposed for a long time, but luckily it didn't get infected.

As well as the farm, Silvio Müller also had a plantation where he grew tobacco. It was many miles away from the house and it was run by his two sons. One weekend, he decided to go there and take Sanata and Cleo with him, which meant I could go home. They dropped me off at the church and I ran to our house as fast as my skinny legs would take me, but there was nobody at home. I panicked and started crying. All sorts of crazy thoughts came into my head. Had they run away? Maybe Antonio got drunk and killed them? Maybe the landowner found out about me and Daniel and forced them to leave. Then my sister came up behind me and made me jump. She said mother was working down by the stream and she asked why I was crying. I felt so silly.

When my mother saw me, she couldn't believe her eyes. A look of concern immediately spread across her face.

'What has happened to you, Rozana?'

'I'm alright.'

'Your head . . . you look so thin!'

I was thin before I left with the Müllers, but by then I was nothing more than skin and bone. My mother made an herb paste and put it on the gash above my eyebrow, but it was too late to prevent the scar I still carry to this day. But none of that mattered to me. I was just happy to be home, even as the third daughter – not counting the one who died – in a poor family, not as a rich girl or a *gringa* or a prodigy. The weekend passed quickly and I was hoping the Müllers wouldn't come back to collect me on the Sunday.

But they did.

My mother didn't want me to go back with them, but I was afraid the policeman would come and put us all in jail. If he thought I'd told anyone about what he threatened, he would shoot me in my feet as well. So I went back to my life of hell.

Later that year, Cleo passed her teaching exams and got her degree. The Müller house was quite isolated and it was surrounded by dense forest with a track road running through it. Cleo was afraid to walk through the woods alone to get to the schoolhouse so I had to walk with her every morning – then go back to do my work before returning to the school in the evening to walk her home. Each trip took an hour and a half, so I was walking for six hours a day, as well as doing my jobs, meaning I finished much later in the evenings.

I was frightened when I had to walk through the forest alone because animals and snakes would move in the bushes and trees and I was constantly terrified of the sound of the wind and of ghosts and demons and escaped murderers. Once a week, I was allowed to stay in the school and take lessons in reading, writing and arithmetic so they could say they were keeping their promise to educate me.

Before I realised it, three years had passed. By the time I turned eleven, I looked and felt like a fifty-year-old woman. I was small and skinny and my breasts had grown out of proportion to the rest of me. My teeth were rotten and my skin was hard and weathered. I always wore a sad expression on my face – a hopeless frown – a gloomy gaze that allowed no sign of laughter or lightness to displace it.

The last year I was there, I only saw my family twice. The second time I came home, my mother was doing her washing by the stream. I sat on a hill and looked down at her. For a while, she didn't notice I was there, then she looked up at me.

'Rozana?'

'It's me, *mãe*.'

'You look like a ghost.'

I was so happy to see her that I couldn't find the words to speak. My voice was stuck in my throat and tears clouded my eyes. There were so many things I wanted to say but, instead, I walked away in silence before she could get close to me. I walked to the *represa* and found my sister and some other children swimming there. They didn't recognise me at first, but I joined them and it was as if I was a child again. I'd forgotten what that feeling was like, to be young and looking forward to the future – or what it was to be free. The feeling of being part of a wider landscape had been driven out of me and all I could see was sorrow.

When I got back home, my mother was cooking a special meal of rice and chicken. She said I could have any part of the chicken I wanted because it was so long since she'd seen me. This made me feel very special. My mother wasn't one to show her true feelings very often so when she did, it meant a lot.

The next day was Sunday and, in the afternoon, I had to go to the church and wait for the Müllers to pick me up. I felt so sad, going back to that life. Again, my mother told me I shouldn't think I had to go, but I was still afraid of what would happen if I didn't.

When I got back to that big house, the ill-treatment continued. I was never paid a single *real* for the work I did and it wasn't long before I became seriously ill. I really needed a doctor or a hospital if I was going to survive. But the Müllers didn't want the bother or expense of having me treated, so they drove me back to Lageado and dumped me in the road. It was dark and I lay there for a long time until someone found me. They didn't recognise me, but I was able to tell them my name They carried me to our hut and my mother took me in her arms. I was so light I was like a doll to her. She put me in one of the beds and waited, unsure of whether I would live or die.

CHAPTER FIVE
PONTA GROSSA

It took me a long time to recover. Many weeks. My parents couldn't afford to stay at home and look after me, so it was left to my younger sister to be my nursemaid – to beg bread for me during the day and to bring me water.

My mother gave me as much food and love as she could in the evenings – more than she gave to the others – to build up my strength. There was no doctor and no medicine and I could easily have followed my brother Joseph and my sister Josephina to the grave.

Yet somehow, I did not.

Gradually, very gradually, I grew stronger. My wasted body came back to the natural thinness it had before the Müllers. I could walk on my skinny legs again, and use the muscles in my scrawny arms. When I got well, the Müllers wanted me back. I was their *criada*. They got me at a young age and believed I would work for them, for free, forever. However, my mother wouldn't allow it. My father was worried in case they caused trouble for us, but she didn't care. I wasn't going back there to work myself to death.

Once I was back to normal health, it felt good to be home, with the rashes and the lice and the worms escaping through my nose. But I was no longer a little girl and I had to do something to help the family.

People heard I was well again and came to the hut to offer me little jobs. For the first time in my life, I was earning some money – and it felt good. As soon as I could, I went with my parents to work on the plantation and in the evenings, I helped my mother with

48

the housework. I was happy to do this. It was certainly better than being a slave.

After a while, I went with my father to the Müllers house to collect my few clothes – the yellow dress and flip-flops and a few other bits and pieces I'd left behind. It took us a long time to walk there and, when we arrived, I could tell the family was angry because they never spoke a single word. Cleo wouldn't even look at my face. I was worried in case her boyfriend showed up. He might shoot me in the feet and shoot my father in the heart. Luckily, he didn't, *graças a Deus,* and the Müllers were not inclined to beat me in front of my father.

And so I left my life of slavery and went back home. Inside though, I knew I wouldn't stay there for long. I'd changed, and they had not. I began to believe again that I had a future, and it lay somewhere else.

After a couple of months, a woman from Ponta Grossa came to Lageado looking for a girl to take care of her baby whilst she and her husband were at work. I wanted to take the job as I was tired of Lageado by then, but my mother was sceptical. She spoke to the woman, whose name was Karina Oliviera. She was born in our village and visited occasionally to see her parents.

'Last time, she nearly died.'

'Who was she working for?'

'Sanata Müller.'

Karina frowned, she obviously knew Sanata Müller.

'I'm not surprised. If she stayed with that witch for three years, she will stay with us forever. We are human beings, not slave drivers.'

So, It was arranged that I could go back with Karina Oliviera to Ponta Grossa.

Karina and I left on a bus from Palmar, which was a village about two hours away from Lageado by foot. The trip took half a day. I had never been in a big city before and I was really excited about going there.

Ponta Grossa was the fourth largest city in the Brazilian state of Paraná, with a population of three hundred thousand. It was also known as the *Princesa dos Campos* – the Princess of the Fields – and it had the *Parque Estadual da Vila Velha*, which was made of rocky formations from millions of years ago. Each rock formation had its own name, depending on what it resembled.

The residents were mainly Brazilian, German or Slavs, although there were also large groups of Russian, Polish, Dutch, Italian, Lebanese and Japanese people. Being in a large city for the first time gave me a huge feeling of achievement. It really felt like the beginning of a new life. Everything was so big – the people, the shops, the buses – and I was so small. From day one, I was so excited at the prospect of becoming part of it. Growing into it.

We got off the main bus from Palmar at about 5:00pm and we took a local bus to the house where Karina lived with her husband, Paulo, and their six-month-old baby, Caio. The area was called Vila Maria and it was a suburban working class district.

The house was small, with only one bedroom, which meant I had to sleep on a sofa in the living room. There was a bathroom with a toilet and a shower and nothing much else, but even this was luxury to me. Though it was a small house, it was nice inside – comfortable, homely and welcoming, not surly and frowning like the Müller's mansion. It was situated on a large piece of land that had been cleared, meaning there were no trees or hedges or grass. When it rained, the ground turned to a mud pit.

There was a railway line nearby and also a convent, which reassured me a little. After being abused by Daniel, I believed I would never get to heaven unless I did a special penance to atone for my sins. I thought about becoming a nun and dedicating my life to God. That way, He might forgive me. Having the convent close by was like a sign, as if my good intentions had been recognised and accepted. But now that I'd been seduced by the city, I didn't wish to be a nun any more. I felt guilty and told God if He gave me another chance, I wouldn't waste it.

Vila Maria looked so different from anywhere I'd lived before. It was so urban and so up-to-date and colourful. I was carrying many scars, both physical and emotional, and I was almost afraid of believing things would work out for me there – but I did hope. I had to. Everything was so wonderful and new, so full of promise.

Karina worked the day-shift on a chicken factory production line and Paulo worked the night-shift in the same place. The company was called Perdigão, a big food producer in southern Brazil. They were both kind to me and I loved looking after little Caio.

Life was good.

Karina would leave for work at 7:00am and Paulo would arrive home from his job shortly after. He would go straight to bed and I would be in charge of the house. I could cook whatever I wanted and do the housework whenever I wanted. When the baby slept, I slept as well. Everything was perfect.

They paid me fifty *reais* a month in arrears and, on my first payday, it felt like I'd won the lottery. I never had so much money before and I didn't know what to do with it. I bought myself a pair of pyjamas and saved the rest so I could go see my mother.

One day, after I'd been there a few weeks, I opened the bathroom door after taking a shower and Paulo was standing outside.

'I'm sorry, Paulo . . . '

'Don't be. I'm in no hurry.'

I wasn't sure how long he was standing there, or why he didn't just knock the door, but I thought nothing of it because I was going home for a few days. Karina's sister had been visiting for a week and I knew her from Lageado. She was going back there and Karina had a few days off work and said I could go with her. I put on my new pyjamas and went down to the bus stop.

Home wasn't the same after being in the city and, when the visit was over, I couldn't wait to get to Ponta Grossa again. Karina went back to work and I was in charge of the house and everything resumed its perfection.

One afternoon while Caio slept, I decided to take a long shower. It was glorious, feeling the warm water falling on my skin. It was a simple thing, a shower, and something most people would take for granted, but to me it was luxury beyond belief. When I was finished, I opened the door to find Paulo standing there again.

'Paulo, have you been there long?'

'Not long. I'm in no hurry.'

The baby was still sleeping and I made a pot of coffee. Paulo bought some fresh bread and we sat at the table chatting. He was a very witty man. He asked all about my family and said Karina was really pleased with my work. He was getting closer while we spoke, but then a neighbour, Alina, came over to borrow something. Caio woke up and Paulo moved back away from me.

Alina had a baby girl who was six-months-old, and she invited me to bring Caio to her house and play with her daughter so Paulo could get some rest.

As time went on, I noticed that Paulo didn't sleep as much as he used to. He would wake up in time to have lunch with me and sometimes he would look after Caio while I had a long shower. After that, I would take the baby to Alina's most afternoons. I couldn't believe how good life was – too good to be true.

One afternoon, I fell asleep on the sofa with Caio. When I awoke, Paulo was sitting opposite, staring at me. I noticed that my dress had ridden up and I pulled it back down, embarrassed. You must understand that I didn't have proper underwear of my own, just castoffs from my sisters that were too big and loose for me. He smiled.

'Don't worry. I see you like that a lot.'

That made me feel uncomfortable.

Later that day, after I had taken my shower, he was waiting outside the bathroom door again.

'I was hoping you would invite me in, Rozana.'

'Why?'

'To have a shower with you.'

I wondered how he could be so interested in a skinny eleven-year-old with rotten teeth like me, especially having such a lovely wife like Karina. It was different with Daniel, he was a boy and what he did to me was out of spite, not lust. Paulo was a man, and I was too young and naive to know that some men had that thing inside them – a primal, animalistic thing tolerated somewhere in history where sexuality was nothing but a restless internal energy and sexual appetite had no connection with merit as a civilised human being.

I walked away without saying a word, but he followed me.

'You're not a virgin, are you?'

I didn't answer.

I found out later that he already knew I was abused by Daniel. That's why he thought I was promiscuous. In Brazil back then, it wasn't uncommon for children from poor families to have sex for money. It was readily available for people who wanted to find it, so he probably thought I'd be easy prey and I wouldn't resist. He grabbed me and pulled me close to him. He wasn't wearing a shirt and I could feel his heart beating very fast. His breath coiled round me like an excited snake. I tried to threaten him with his wife.

'I'll tell Karina.'

'She won't believe you.'

Maybe she would. Maybe he had tried this with other girls.

'If you say anything, I'll tell her you came on to me. Who do you think she'll believe?'

He was right. There was no way on earth she'd believe me over him. I pulled away from him and went to the baby. I could tell the rejection angered him. It was a macho thing with Brazilian men, they believed every woman was just waiting to have sex with them. If not, she was either a lesbian or an idiot. To be rejected was an insult to their sense of manhood, even if the girl or woman did nothing to encourage them. To be rejected by a poor *negrinha* girl like me was a huge blow to his ego – one that he wouldn't get over easily.

The next day I told Karina I wanted to go home, but she said there was no one to take me and she couldn't get any time off work for at least two months. From that day onwards, Paulo pestered me unmercifully. He would touch me by pretending to put his arms round the baby while I was holding him and let his hand slip to my breast. He would try to get me to touch him and say disgusting things that made me feel cheap and dirty, all the while making him feel macho. I would do my work as fast as I could, rush round to Alina's with the baby and stay there until Karina came home.

My dream had again turned into a nightmare, so I decided the only thing to do was to run away as soon as I got paid at the end of the month.

But, when payday came, Paulo dangled the money in front of me.

'Do you want this?'

'Of course. I earned it.'

'Then you have to sleep with me.'

'No.'

'Then I'll use this money to pay a prostitute.'

He wanted me to try to get the money from him, then he would have an excuse to grab me and touch me and try to have sex with me. But God was giving me another chance and I didn't want to squander it, so I didn't even attempt to take the money. Instead, I tried to get out of the house. Paulo came after me and, when he caught me, he ripped my top. I pushed him and a piece of my shirt came away in his hand. Then I made a run for it and scrambled round to Alina's house, leaving the baby behind so he couldn't follow me.

I was upset and sobbing and Alina wanted to know what happened. I told her what was going on and that Paulo tried to rape me. She believed me because she could see my T-shirt was torn and I had scratches on my arms.

When Karina came round to Alina's, she was very angry and wanted to fight with me because she believed I'd tried to seduce her husband. I couldn't understand how she could believe something like that, but then some women are very gullible when it comes to their husbands. Or maybe they just don't want to accept the truth because it would be too painful for them.

In any case, Alina took my side and explained to Karina what really happened, while I stayed in the bedroom with her baby girl, in case Karina tried to hit me. Karina was shouting and saying I was a liar, claiming I used to sleep with people in Lageado. Alina couldn't calm her down or convince her of the truth, but after half an hour of screaming she left, and I never saw her again.

Alina let me stay at her house for a few nights and, in return, I helped her with the baby and the housework. But she couldn't afford to keep me, so I eventually decided to go back home.

By the time I arrived in Lageado, everyone was talking about me. They were saying I was nothing better than a prostitute for trying to seduce a married man. Karina's sister had spread the word around the village. I was a total embarrassment. Everybody shunned me and I wasn't even allowed to go to church because they believed I was tainted.

My mother tried to pretend everything was alright, but I could see she was embarrassed because everyone was talking and pointing their fingers. There was more malicious gossip in the places where Antonio was drinking, so he would come home and be more violent than ever, blaming me and calling me a whore. True to form, my father just completely ignored the situation. He closed his ears to the noise and dreamed his dreams in a place where nothing could get to him. After a couple of weeks of this ostracism, I couldn't take it any longer. I had no alternative. I was full of shame and had to leave.

I'd let God down again.

I walked the two hours to the village of Palmar and took the bus. I had no idea what I was going to do or where I was going to go. Maybe I could just knock on doors and look for work and a place to stay.

Anything.

Just to get away.

CHAPTER SIX
PUBERTY

After travelling on the bus as far as my *reais* would take me, I arrived in a farming area that I hadn't been to before. As I hadn't had any better ideas, I went knocking on doors in search of a job.

I was an outcast, all alone, but that worked in my favour for once because I didn't want anyone to know who I'd become – a bad girl who seduced her employer's husband.

My middle name is Janislei, so I became Jane with no surname, and after walking for miles and miles, I finally got a job with the Galvão family. The wife was called Elvina and she was pregnant. Her maiden name was Shereiner and she was of German descent. The husband's name was Sami, who was Arabian, and there was a mother-in-law called Delores who lived with them.

They had a pig farm and a little shop with a communal telephone. My job was to work with the pigs, help out in the shop and look after the baby when it was born. I told them I was twenty-years-old – I looked it, even though I hadn't yet turned twelve – with no background and no story to tell.

I didn't want Elvina to know about my past, how I was promiscuous and loose. She'd be afraid I would tempt her husband and she'd tell me to leave. They liked the idea of me being anonymous because, if I had no family, there would be nowhere for me to go and I wouldn't need any time off. They didn't pay me wages, just gave me food and castoff clothing.

They lived in a very old farmhouse and I slept in the loft. I wasn't allowed to use the family bathroom and I had to wash outside under a makeshift shower that only had cold water. The toilet was a hole in the ground and it attracted rats, as did the slurry I had to make up for the pigs.

The Galvãos were in their late thirties, which was old in Brazil to be having a first baby. She came from a wealthy family in Maringá – the third largest city in the State of Paraná – who had a chain of garages. But her brother got involved in crime and killed someone, so most of their money went paying his legal bills. The family of the man he killed set fire to the garages and burned them down. They weren't insured, so Elvina had to marry Sami the pig farmer.

I ate whatever the family ate, but I had to sit in a separate room. The mother-in-law was the hardest on me. She complained that I was a disgusting, ignorant *mendiga* with no manners. It's a thing with Brazilians if they have more than you, they think they're better than you and they let you know it. Maybe it was the same elsewhere, but to me it just seemed to be embedded in the Brazilian psyche, stemming from a flawed code of morals and a national psychosis about success, along with an illusive and mistaken notion of what success really was.

There were two nice things about the job. The first was a really pretty stream that ran past the end of a big field at the edge of the pig farm. I used to walk there and daydream, like my father. The second was books. Elvina was a teacher in a modest local primary school and she kept a lot of books in the house. I was allowed to read them when I had the time and I took full advantage of this privilege, using every spare minute to do so. This greatly improved my imagination and broadened my horizons and my outlook on life.

There were story books with homework, which I interpreted in my own way and let my mind fly away over the forest and the hills. I didn't have any problems with Sami, not like with Paulo in Ponta Grossa. He hardly spoke to me except to give me orders and I think he saw me more as a little beast of burden rather than an actual human being. As long as I completed my work, I could do whatever

I liked – read the books or stroll by the magical stream and dream.

I stayed with the Galvãos for two anonymous years, until I was over thirteen. During this time, I missed my mother and I regretted leaving the way I did. I constantly worried that she'd think I was dead. The longer I stayed away, the more I thought about her, and that only made me miss her more. I wondered if she'd put my younger brother, José, up for adoption, like she always jokingly threatened to do.

All the while I couldn't say anything, of course, because the Galvãos believed I had no family. I was the girl from nowhere and that's exactly how I felt, like I didn't belong anywhere in this world. I longed for someone to love; to love me, not desire me. If someone had, I would have loved them back unconditionally. I would have traded my love for theirs for as long as they wanted it. Even after they stopped wanting it, I would still have continued to give it. I saw myself as a tiny, irrelevant speck in the huge maelstrom of humanity, spinning around and being blown hither and thither like a feather in a gale, not knowing where I would eventually end up.

There was a church close to the pig farm that I attended every Sunday with the family, and a dirt road went right past it. I always wondered what was down the road and, one day after I'd finished my work, I decided to take a look. I walked and walked, like I was in a trance, past numerous houses, fields and farms – losing track of distance and time – thinking about my mother, my family and my future. I was oblivious to the time slipping by until I noticed that night was approaching. I had walked miles from the Galvão's pig farm and I'd never be able to get back before it became so dark I wouldn't be able to see. When it got dark in rural Brazil, it got pitch black – no light whatsoever if it was overcast; no moon or stars to see by.

I was afraid of being eaten by some animal or being spirited away by a *Curupira* or the *Lobisomen* and I didn't know what to do. I thought about climbing a tree and staying there until it got light, but snakes could climb trees. I considered covering myself over in the undergrowth, but poisonous spiders and other dangers lurked there.

'Rozana, what are you doing here?'

I whirled around, startled. A girl called Claudette, who I knew from going to the church, had come up behind me.

'Claudette, it's you!'

'Of course it's me. Why are you here in the dark?'

'I went for a walk, but it got too late.'

'You can stay at my house.'

She was on her way home and she took me with her. I stayed the night and as soon as it got light, I made my way quickly back to the Galvãos. They were very angry and had looked everywhere for me – in the fields and the forest, behind the farm and along the stream where I used to walk. How inconsiderate of me to stay out all night. After all, they were responsible for me!

In actual fact, they considered that they owned me, like their pigs. They told me I'd have to leave because I was too irresponsible. They couldn't trust me anymore. All I had done was go for a walk. It was a long walk, but in doing that I'd shown some independence. What on earth might I do next? I was dangerous because I thought for myself, even if it was in a very limited way.

The Galvãos weren't bad people. They believed I had no family and they were doing good by helping me. It was just the system; the culture. I was a good worker, but that was all I would ever be to them. They couldn't think of me as anything else, certainly not their equal. And they would never see the seething, swirling firmament in the background behind them – just themselves, standing smugly in the foreground.

In a way, I was pleased to have to leave. I'd been gone two years and it was time for a change. I'd had enough of working for nothing and I needed to move on, but first I had to see my mother again. Elvina gave me a few *reais* for the bus and I wandered by the pretty stream for hours before mustering enough courage to go home again.

By 1986 they were building a new motorway, which made the journey quicker and easier. On the way I passed the *Castello*, which looked like a castle where young homeless girls and runaways would go to prostitute themselves for passing lorry drivers – and I knew my life could be worse than it was. The new bus route took me closer to Lageado, closer than Palmar, but it was still late in the evening when I got home. My hands were clammy and my mouth was dry with anticipation.

The first person I saw was my sister.

'Hello, Celia.'

'I'm not Celia. I'm Nicole.'

'Oh my God!'

It was my younger sister, not my older sister as I thought. She looked so grown up. There was a lump in my throat and I wanted to cry. She just laughed.

'Rozana, is it you?'

'Yes, it's me.'

My mother was sitting on the floor, peeling butternut squash when I went into the hut. I sat on the floor opposite her and she looked at me. I could tell she was emotional – half angry, half relieved. Angry because I left without telling her where I was going and she probably thought I was dead, but relieved because I wasn't. She was searching for words to say.

'I thought you had forgotten us.'

'I could never do that.'

'You came on a bad day. This is all we have to eat.'

Then she stood up and went outside. I was hurt. I wanted her to hug me and say how glad she was that I'd come back. I followed her out.

'*Mãe* . . .'

'How long are you staying this time?'

The tone of her voice was strange – alien to me. It was almost as if she didn't want me there. I thought at first that it might still be the stigma of the malicious rumours about me and Paulo, but it wasn't. Everyone had forgotten about that. It was just my mother's inability to communicate her real feelings. She had to put her hard side out to the world. It was the only way she could survive.

In a naive way, I kept going back because I saw myself as my family's salvation. They were stuck in time, not moving forward like I thought I was. I saw it as my responsibility to show them the way. They'd gotten used to being the poorest people in the village, on the lowest rung of the social ladder, and they were afraid of trying anything else.

On the other hand, I had changed. I had dreams. I wanted to study. I wanted to have money. I wanted to be like the people I saw on television. Without me to show them what could be achieved, they would be lost forever. That's what I honestly believed and it was one of the reasons I kept going back. The other reason was, of course, that things weren't working out for me either and I had no choice.

There was a little square mirror hanging on the wall. I used to dance in front of it and tell them I was going to be on television, like the people in the soap operas that they'd never seen, but I had. Like the people in the stories of the books I'd read, but they hadn't. I tried to make them dream like me, but they didn't know how. They laughed at me and thought I was going mad. It made me sad and, after a few weeks, I gave up trying and decided to leave again.

I wanted a job that would facilitate me going to school. If I could get that, I was willing to work just for food. I went to Palmar first, but could find nothing there. However, I heard through a friend of Sami the pig farmer that a woman in Imbituva was looking for a girl with experience. I got the address and took the bus there.

Imbituva was a sophisticated town and, while it wasn't as sprawling as Ponta Grossa, it was very compact and middle-class.

There were no really poor areas and there were lots of factories, churches, colleges, shops, big houses, expensive bars and rich kids with flash cars. The factories made cardigans and laminated floors and the people had beach homes that they visited on weekends.

The woman's name was Lourdes Melani and her husband was Nelson. They were both over sixty and had a son called Rick, who was twenty-two, and they lived in a three-bedroom house above a clothes factory. The job was easy enough. I had to clean the house and do the washing and ironing. They promised to send me to school, but I didn't have immediate access to the education I wanted, which was a disappointment.

The house in Imbituva was old, but comfortable enough. I had my own room and was allowed to use the bathroom and eat with the family. My childhood rashes had disappeared and Lourdes bought me a comb to get rid of the nits from my hair. But I still had the worms that slithered around inside my belly.

I was thirteen and I was jealous of the rich kids. I wanted to be like them and for that to happen, I knew I would have to go back to school. I would have to learn how to use my brain better than I had been. I was considered clever during the previous periods I was able to take lessons and I knew I could be as good as anyone else if I could just get a chance to show it. An education shouldn't have been a privilege for the rich, but the right of everybody. My social conscience was developing and I began to see proportion rather than distortion.

After I'd been with the Melanis for three or four months, they said that Rick had passed his exams and they were going to move to Maringá so he could get a job at a hospital that was run by their rich family. Maringá was seven hours away from Lageado by bus and I didn't want to move that distance from home in case anything happened and I had to get back again.

They never paid me any money for the work I did, so I had no bus fare to go anywhere else. To be honest, I didn't want to go back to Lageado either. There was nothing for me there, so I knew I would have to go – and keep going.

To follow my dreams.

The love and attachment I felt for my mother would have to be left somewhere else until I could pick it up again; put to the back of my mind until I could live without it no longer. I could read, write, add, subtract, divide and multiply, but I wanted to do more. I wanted to look like the people on television with nice hair and good teeth and no worms. My destiny was somewhere else, not in Lageado or Palmar or Ponta Grossa or Imbituva.

Maybe it was in Maringá?

If you were poor like me in Brazil, it was quite normal for the family you worked for to think of you as part of their furniture. To them, you had no feelings, no emotions, no ambitions. Therefore, if they moved, you moved with them. So, in July 1986, I began a new life in Maringá.

I was still only thirteen and Maringá was a different world, bigger than Imbituva or Ponta Grossa, full of soaring skyscrapers, television channels, radio stations, shopping malls, Coca-Cola and very rich people.

The two-bedroom house we moved to was in a suburb called Borba Gato. It was a new suburb where a lot of houses were being built. Ours was not completely finished, so I had to sleep in the toilet for a while. It was very hot in there, over forty degrees, with just a small window for ventilation and a curtain for a door. If somebody wanted to go during the night, I would have to wake up and wait outside. Then I'd have to go back into the stifling smell of sweat and excrement, but there was nothing I could do about it.

As time went by, I was getting really anxious about my education.

'When am I going to start school, Lourdes?'

'Stop asking me stupid questions, Rozana.'

'But, I want to learn . . . '

'Why? People like you are never going to get anywhere.'

Lourdes Melani was not a bad person, she was just like the rest of the middle-class who believed us *camponeses* were born to serve them and nothing else, but I needed more than that from my life. I had no one to hug, no one to love – I had to have an outlet for the emotions inside me.

The Melani family didn't understand. How could someone who was little more than an animal have emotions? To keep my mind focused, I began to write poetry.

Broken Wings

Yesterday, I could fly
Wings touching air and sky
World so small from up high
Blue and green in my eye

Today I just sit and cry
Kissed my broken wings goodbye
Hopelessness within my sigh
Life will never satisfy

To rise up from where I lie
The sweet air will not deny
Tomorrow I will again try
My flight from grub to butterfly

The verses were simple and naive at first. Sometimes Lourdes would go into my room and read what I'd written and I could hear her laughing. She would tell Nelson and say she was worried for my sanity. Gradually, though, the poems became more complex and sophisticated – and the more they believed I was mad, the more determined I became to show them I wasn't.

Cansada

Eu preciso ir, cansei de esperar . . .
Cansei de amar sem ser amada.
Estou sem forças para chorar e
Sem vontade de sorrir.

Eu perdi a fé ... cansei de querer
Fiquei sem animo pra tentar denovo.
Não quero mais recomeçar . . .
Vou sair agora antes que você volte . . .

Se alguem perguntar por mim,
Não precisa mentir . . .
Apenas fale, que cansei! Perdi o animo!
Fiquei sem força, perdi a fé . . .

There was a girl my age who lived opposite. Her name was Monica and we had similar interests like music, dancing and a deep teenage crush on a man called Rudolfo. He was twenty-seven years old and worked as a presenter on a popular radio programme called *Jornal.* Of all the men on television and radio, I don't know why I should have fallen so heavily for him. It was something indefinable, something magnetic.

If I could only be with him, all my dreams would come true.

I became totally obsessed with this man and I wanted him to show me things – not sexual things, more than that. Hope. I wanted him to show me hope and to make me feel alive. More than alive. Eternal. Part of everything. With him.

He was more than a man, or maybe he wasn't and it was just that the others I'd experienced were less than men. I believed he could teach me how to love and laugh and live and listen – how to be a real woman, not a fake sterile cipher – a woman with a deeper light, a more profound identity. Rudolfo would make me that kind of woman. If I could just get close to him. He was many things in Brazilian society, a lawyer and politician and media presenter, who just so happened to be well educated, handsome and rich.

To me he was iconic, a shining star that was more than a human being. I knew he would be kind, understanding, philosophical and magnanimous. Just like God. However, I realised that if I wanted to be with Rudolfo, I had to do something about my appearance – especially my teeth and the worms. There was a dental practise in the suburb that offered free treatment for the first ten people to arrive each day.

The doors opened at 9:00am.

On the first day, I was there at 6:00am, but there was already a queue of more than ten people. The next morning, I arrived at 5:00am, but still found over ten people queuing. I came at 4:00am the following morning, but still could not get into the first ten. When I came at 3:00am, I managed to get a place. The treatment took forty-minutes each morning, with thirty-minutes to walk back to start my work by 10:00am. I was always rushing, trying not to be late, always tired from being up at 3:00am and queuing for six hours. The dentist was a trainee and the anaesthetic didn't work well because my teeth were so rotten.

'Tell me if it hurts and I'll stop.'

It hurt a lot, but I thought he meant he would stop treating me altogether, so I said nothing, just held on tight to the arms of the dentist chair and put up with the excruciating pain. He could only do one tooth at a time and I went twice a week. The Melanis thought it was a stupid thing for me to do and they had no sympathy for me. It took three months altogether. I had no painkillers and my mouth felt like it was constantly on fire.

But, at the end of the treatment, I had a new smile.

Then my mouth became infected. There was no medicine to treat the infection and I was worried in case my new teeth would have to be taken back out, so I didn't complain. After a few weeks of intense suffering, the infection cleared up of its own accord. My beautiful smile gave me a new confidence and after what I had been through to get it, I began to believe I could do anything.

The dental clinic also gave me some medicine that finally got rid of my worms and I felt like a new person. I'd been born again – a new Rozana Ramos was rising from the ashes of the old one. My friend Monica encouraged me and, behind the Melanis' backs, she took me to a free education institution. They gave me an assessment to see what level I was at and I came out at year five, which was the standard for twelve-year-olds. This was good news and was due to the sporadic learning I'd had previously. I could start evening classes at that level in the local *segundo grau* school as soon as I turned fourteen.

The Melanis had to approve, of course, as they were responsible for me. I didn't think they would but, to my surprise, they did. They were astounded that someone like me could achieve that much. Maybe I wasn't entirely ignorant or stupid. Maybe I was more than a half-human little *negrinha,* after all.

I did well at school and made many new friends. Life was good again. In 1987 there was a poetry contest that I entered and won. This made me eligible to go on and represent the school at the state-wide competition, the winner of which would be interviewed by Rudolfo. But the Melanis refused to let me go because it was in the city centre and it would have interfered with my work. I think the real reason was they believed it would open doors for me and I would get above my station, jeopardising their hold over me. They would have to find another little slave to work for them for free, so the girl who came second in the contest went on to represent the school at state level instead of me. The biggest disappointment was not being able to go on the radio station to be interviewed by Rudolfo as winner.

It made me cry.

I became difficult to manage, telling the Melanis that Rudolfo loved me and was going to marry me because I was best in my class – that I was different from the other students and that I had a brilliant future ahead of me. They didn't want to listen to this, but I kept on and on about it.

After getting my new teeth and ridding myself of worms, they were bringing me back down. I started to get depressed and had severe mood swings. I heard them talking, asking how I could believe someone like Rudolfo would have anything to do with someone like me, but I blamed them for depriving me of the chance to meet him. They had mouse poison in the house and I got so dejected I swallowed half a bottle. It made me really sick. I was vomiting for three or four days and suffered from stomach pains for weeks.

It was my first true suicide attempt.

But I survived and that made me more depressed than ever. I wanted them to know how badly they hurt me and I put the milk from a plant called *corora de cristo*, which supposedly made people blind, into my eyes. It didn't make me completely blind, but the milk dried like glue and everything was blurry, so I couldn't see properly and the pain was horrific.

Lourdes was angry and made me do my work anyway. I dropped a bucket full of water and broke it, so she sent me to a local surgery on my own. I was half blind and bumping into trees and things on the way. They washed my eyes and gave me drops and I got better. After that, I burned my hands with a hot iron and that was the last straw for the Melanis. They decided I was mad and they would have to take me back to my family. I didn't want to go there because, all the emotions aside, I was finally getting somewhere – and I had only just managed to store my love for my mother away in a place that I couldn't easily find it.

But I had no money, and therefore no choice.

For one reason or another, I was going backwards time and time again.

CHAPTER SEVEN
MARINGÁ

In Lageado, things were just the same.

It was like I'd never left.

I went back to work on the plantation until I could save enough money for the bus fare back to Maringá. I couldn't be away from Rudolfo for too long in case he found somebody else to love; in case he gave his heart to another woman while I was away. It had to be me and no one else – or I would die.

Maringá was divided into Zones from one to seven – the lower the Zone, the richer the area. Rudolfo lived close to Zone One, in an area called *Alameda dos Magnatas*.

All the rich people had domestic servants who lived close by in small annexes on the land of their employers. I was lucky and quickly found a place to live with a woman who was a friend of the family of a girl I knew from the free school. She was a single mother with two children and the only house rule was that I had to be in by 10:30pm. She wouldn't give me my own key and didn't want to be disturbed after that time. So all I needed was a job.

I started knocking on doors, looking for the kind of work I was used to, but nobody was hiring. Then I went into a beauty salon and asked if they needed a cleaner. The woman's name was Dulce and she didn't need a cleaner, but she did need a manicurist.

'I have no experience.'

'I'll teach you.'

Dulce's child had died of a lung infection and I think she saw me as a substitute because I looked so forlorn and vulnerable. However, the first customers I worked on left with their fingers bleeding because I cut the cuticles down too far. So Dulce sent me on a beautician course to improve my skills.

Working in the city centre was perfect for me. The salon was close to the radio station where Rudolfo had his show, so I started seeing one of the security guards in order to get access. He was much older than me, maybe forty or so. He was lanky, skinny and by definition, ugly. He wanted to have sex with me but I kept putting him off. In the end, he got fed up of trying and didn't want to know me anymore.

This was after he got me access to the radio station though, and I let them know I was the one who won the poetry competition the previous year. Rudolfo wasn't there, so I didn't get to see him, but they were very surprised to discover I was the one who had actually won and not the girl they interviewed. They felt sorry for me because I'd been denied the opportunity to go to the state competition, so they decided to interview me anyway because it was a good human interest story. After the interview, they said I came across very natural and professional and they asked if I would like to present a show for them.

Of course I would!

I jumped at the chance to be working close to Rudolfo and have him as a colleague before he became my lover and my husband.

The show was called *Sinfonia Da Saudade* and it was an interactive cultural slot with a subject for the day and guest appearances. I took calls from listeners and read poetry. I didn't get paid, but that didn't matter. I loved it. I'd gone from a wandering waif to a radio poetry presenter. That's how fast life could change – but if it could change so quickly one way, it could also change quickly for the worse.

I still couldn't get to meet Rudolfo because, before I started, he won an election and became a *Deputado Estadual* and moved to Curitiba, the capital city of Paraná. Then he got married in a big, glamorous service to a famous lawyer and gave up his radio career. I knew he couldn't possibly love her and that he only married her to further his career. If I could only get to meet him, he would see that I was his true soul-mate. *I* was the meaning of his life, the source of his inspiration, his talisman, his tau. It could only be me – only me! Could it not – God?

I kept ringing his office but only got through to his secretary. I rang and rang and rang, without any luck. Then, one day, he answered the phone himself.

'Hello.'

I was startled. I was *finally* speaking to him personally, and I didn't know what to say.

'Who's there?'

'Emm, Rudolfo . . . I was just ringing in the hope of speaking to you personally. I'm sorry, I don't mean to intrude. I'm somebody who is very fond of you.'

My words were fast and nervous – stammering – stumbling out of my mouth.

'Calm down, Charlene. Calm down.'

Rudolfo had a girlfriend called Charlene before he got married. She was a model. My voice must have sounded like hers on the phone because he obviously thought it was her. I decided to pretend I was Charlene and spent the next two hours telling him how much I loved him. In return, he opened his heart to me and said he loved me too, and that he'd only married his wife for the politics. This, of course, I already knew, and I knew he didn't love Charlene either. It was *me* he loved. Why else did he give me his private number and ask me to use that one in the future?

Which I did, every day, for the next two months.

I got to know everything about him and he kept saying we should meet, but how could I do that? He would be expecting Charlene, who was tall and blonde with blue eyes. Instead, I would be there – Rozana Ramos, five foot nothing, with dark hair and brown eyes. But sooner or later, we would have to meet if my destiny was going to fulfil itself. I couldn't continue pretending forever.

Then, one day when I called, his voice sounded different.

'Somebody here wants to talk to you.'

'Hello . . .'

'Hello! Who's this?'

It was the real Charlene. I hung up immediately and fell into despair for the next few days. I'd lost my lover before he even became my lover. How would I ever get to meet him now? How would I be able to convince him I was his kismet, his karma? He would despise me for my deception.

Life lost its meaning for a while. It became bland and contourless, but it was busy at least, so I didn't have time to dwell on my despondency. I worked all day in the salon and, in the evenings, I went to the radio station to present the show. I also wrote a letter to my mother, saying I hated her. I hoped she would hate me back and not worry or care about me any more so I could forget about my family and stop going back there and starting all over again. In truth, I knew she'd never hate me, no matter what I said – and she'd know I didn't really hate her, either.

I never sent that letter.

One day, I heard on the radio that Rudolfo was back in Maringá and he was having dinner in the restaurant of a local hotel. It was my opportunity to finally meet him.

I couldn't let it pass.

I was delirious in my obsession and I left the radio station before my show started and rushed to the hotel, but they wouldn't let me in. I waited outside for a long, long time, but he didn't come out. It was midnight before I even realised it. I'd completely forgotten about my show and it was nearly 1:00am when I finally got home. I'd broken the house rule and the woman I lived with was waiting for me with my meagre belongings packed. She wanted to get rid of me anyway and this was her opportunity. I think she was jealous of my radio show and fed up with me talking about it – along with how I was going to marry Rudolfo, even though he was already married to someone else.

I found myself on the street again, in what was a very dangerous area. I was really nervous about being alone in the dark with nowhere to go. I saw the lights of an all-night garage and decided it would be safer to hang about there. The night-attendant was a man called Samuel. He saw me standing around outside for a long time and so he came over.

'Are you alright?'

'No. I've been evicted.'

'They'll think you're a prostitute if you keep standing here.'

'I have nowhere else to go.'

There was an out-of-order toilet at the back of the garage and he told me I could sleep there for the night. The toilet was dirty and full of rubbish because it wasn't being used. There was no light and cobwebs hung from everywhere, so I was unable to sleep, but it was safer than standing outside. Samuel came for me at 5:00am because I had to be out before the day shift people arrived. He was a kind man, a gentleman, and he asked why I was on the streets. I told him I'd been thrown out because I missed my curfew and he was sympathetic. He said he would ask his mother-in-law if I could stay with her.

I left the garage with Samuel and he took me to a development area called *Jardin Universo*, where poor people could erect their own makeshift shacks. The houses were all crowded together, made from tin and wood and other bits and pieces. They looked like rows of dishevelled drunks, propping each other up.

His mother-in-law's house was made of cardboard and the rain came in. She and her husband were in their fifties and they had four sons and two daughters, all between the ages of seventeen and twenty-five. The house and its people were very dirty and there were flies and fleas everywhere. The woman said I could stay, for one hundred *reais* a month. I had nowhere else to go, so I agreed.

I went to work in the salon as normal and, that evening, I went back to the radio station. My producer was called Geni and she was incredibly angry. She'd had to use a recording the night before and she accused me of lacking the commitment she demanded from her presenters, so she cancelled my contract.

I was devastated. Even though I wasn't being paid, I loved my job at the radio station. It was my connection to the finer things in life in what was otherwise an ugly, materialistic world. I felt betrayed. Let down. It made me cry, but there was nothing I could do about it. Things had changed again, quickly, and I only had my own obsession to blame – my wanting – my conviction that I was entitled to something I didn't deserve, or even need.

I slept with the two girls, but they never used sanitary towels and when they had their periods, there would be blood all over the bed and the rain would spread it everywhere. The kitchen was the most disgusting place I'd ever seen. The homemade wooden table had gaps and cracks in it, where bits of food had got lodged and remained, rotting and rancid. What fell onto the floor was never cleaned up and the cooker was covered in sticky grease and dirt. The toilet was outside. It had no roof and it stank, with slugs and maggots crawling up my legs whenever I went in there – but it was better than living on the streets.

I continued to live in the hovel in *Jardin Universo* by night and work in the salon in the city centre by day. One evening when I was returning after work, I met Samuel as he was leaving his house across the road to go to his night shift at the garage. I hadn't seen him since he helped me and it was the first opportunity I had to thank him. We stood talking for a while when, suddenly, his wife came out of the house and started screaming at me.

'You slept with my husband at the garage!'

'No. . .'

'Don't lie to me!'

'I didn't.'

'Liar!'

Samuel tried to protest, but she wouldn't listen to him. I don't know who told her that lie and could only assume it was one of her sisters who I was sharing a bed with and who wanted to get rid of me. The wife stormed across the road to her mother's house and started to throw my clothes out through the door. I was homeless again, without having done anything to deserve it.

While it was still light, I went knocking on the doors of the servants who worked for the rich people in Zone One, but none of them could take me in because of conditions in their work contracts. Night was closing in on me and I couldn't go back to Samuel's garage again. There were public toilets close to the salon where I worked and I knew the old lady who cleaned them. Her nickname was "Nega" and she was friendly to me whenever we had occasion to talk. I went there and asked her if I could sleep in the toilets until I found somewhere to live. Luckily, she agreed.

The toilets were closed from 8:00pm to 6:00am, so I was locked in. It was an eerie place to be at night, knowing that I couldn't get out even if I needed to. The plumbing made strange noises and small, watery echoes followed me round corners and kept me company in the night – but it was clean and Nega had a little cooker in one of the cubicles.

I lived in the public toilets for several weeks, until I met a woman called Vera in the salon. She was about eighteen and married to a man called Carlos, who was a butcher and never spoke very much. Vera was quite cultured so we talked about poetry, music and art and discovered we were like kindred spirits. She was also in love with Rudolfo, even though she was married to Carlos, and she used to hang around the green area that surrounded the rich complex in the hope of meeting him some day.

I told her I was living in the public toilets and she sympathetically invited me to stay in her charming little house until I found myself somewhere else. Needless to say, I was delighted. I hadn't lived in a decent place for a long time and it was like being part of a proper family again. Vera was a good friend and Carlos was a kind man, even though he rarely said anything. I worked all day at the salon and, in the evenings, Vera and I had long conversations into the night. At weekends we cooked together and played games like monopoly and went for walks in the green area around the rich complex to see if we could meet Rudolfo, even though he had moved to Curitiba.

We never saw him, but life was good again for a few months.

As usual, it didn't last.

I came home from work one evening to find Vera looking really sad. I immediately knew something was wrong. She said the landlord had found out I was living there and told her she had to get rid of me or she and Carlos would be evicted. She said I could stay until I found somewhere else, but I didn't want to put them in jeopardy and have all three of us out on the streets. So I went back to the public toilets and lived with the echoes for the next two months.

Then an old lady called Donna Natalia came into the salon to have her nails done. She was over seventy and had a face that would frighten small children, but her sense of humour was extraordinary. During our small-talk, it came out that she was looking for a companion to live with her because she was afraid of being alone in her house.

I moved in the very same day.

She wasn't rich, but she was financially independent and she had a nice three-bedroom house in a suburb called *Nei Braga*, which was about an hour by local bus from the city centre. I had my own room, free use of the bathroom and no rent to pay. She would always have eaten by the time I got in from work, but she would have my dinner ready for me on a plate. It was perfect.

My luck had changed again.

Donna Natalia was a very kind woman. She'd been married three times and had three grown-up daughters, each with their own family. We would go and visit them on weekends and they always made me feel like one of them.

Sometimes, I would have to work late in the salon to cater for our clients' schedules, and I wouldn't get home until maybe 10:00pm. Donna Natalia didn't like this because she was afraid of ghosts and she kept asking me to find another job. Eventually, I did find one, just up the road from where we lived, and I was able to be home by 7:00pm every evening. This pleased her greatly.

The new job was working for a couple who had recently moved to Maringá from São Paulo, the largest city in Brazil. The husband was called Jamie Orlandini and he was a hairdresser. His wife was Zylu and she was a teacher. They had three children who were aged five, ten and seventeen. Zylu taught in São Paulo and she lived there Monday to Friday, coming home on weekends. I worked with Jamie in the salon that was situated at the front of their house. It was a huge house, with an extension to the back.

The children were looked after by a girl called Lucy who came from a similar background to me. She had no family and was thrown out of her previous job for wearing her boss' nightdress. The woman was supposed to be away, but came home early and found Lucy wearing the nightdress, so she threw her out. Lucy slept on the street that night and, as it was across the road from the salon, Jamie found her next morning and gave her the job looking after his children. I saw Lucy's boss throwing the nightdress in the dustbin, so I went across and took it out and kept it. I mean, it was mine if nobody else wanted it – was it not?

The salon was new in the suburb and we didn't have many clients, so I helped Lucy with her work when I wasn't busy. One day she left, without saying a word to anyone. She just disappeared. Jamie asked if I could cover for her until he found someone else. I agreed, but whenever he went out in the evening, I had to stay with the children, sometimes even sleeping over. This wasn't working for Donna Natalia and she gave me an ultimatum: be home by

7:00pm every day or she would get someone else to be her live-in companion. I spoke to Jamie about it and he said the salon wasn't doing very well, so if I couldn't help with the children, I wouldn't be any use to him.

What could I do?

Jamie said I could live with him and Zylu as they had plenty of room in the big house. I loved living with Donna Natalia, but I had to put my job first.

It was Mother's Day the week before I left her house and she asked me to blow-dry her hair before visiting her daughters. I didn't have a hair dryer of my own, so I borrowed one from the salon without telling Jamie. When I told her I was leaving, Donna Natalia got angry and, to punish me, she took the hair dryer to the salon and told Jamie I stole it.

Luckily, he didn't believe her and I explained that I just borrowed it with every intention of bringing it back. Zylu, however, was a different matter. She was extremely religious and self-righteous and believed she was possessed by God when she went to church. She happened to be there when Donna Natalia brought the dryer back and I could tell she wasn't happy, even though she said nothing at the time.

So I left Donna Natalia and moved in with the Orlandinis. As soon as I came to live there, Zylu insisted I should go to her church every weekend. Some men started coming to the house to prepare me for entering the Mormon faith. I didn't want to. I was Catholic.

But I was not given a choice.

CHAPTER EIGHT
THE MORMONS

They were young men, even though they called themselves "elders." Elder Lamb was American and spoke very little Portuguese. Elder George was Brazilian and interpreted for him. Their mission was to bring people into the Mormon Church.

I was one of those people.

They preached the doctrine to me and told me to accept Jesus. They baptised me in a tin bath at the back of the church and they took ten percent of everything I earned, which was very little to begin with. Less than the skinny minimum wage.

But I was "reborn."

I didn't mind at first. I needed something to love because I didn't have my mother or Rudolfo, so Jesus was as good as anything else. I really wanted to feel I was a child of their God, that I belonged with them, that I was part of them – but I never was. I was outside them, thinking my own thoughts, dreaming my own dreams and believing my own lies and imaginings. I was only one of them while it was convenient, while I needed somewhere to kneel and pray. Service was every Sunday from 8:00am till 12 noon and if I didn't feel like going, the elders came and got me.

Then a competition came on the radio: answer ten questions correctly and you could win a horse ride with Menudo, a Puerto Rican boy-band that included Ricky Martin and Draco Rosa. Even more amazing, the horse ride would take place in the grounds of Rudolfo's mansion. It was a miracle – I could win it. I knew I could. It was free to enter and I just needed the time off to go to the radio station and wait for hours in the queue with the others who shared my anticipation of victory – but Zylu wouldn't let me go.

'I can't afford to spare you for hours and hours, and all for nothing Rozana. You won't win, you probably won't even be selected to take part.'

'Please, Zylu. Please. Please. Please.'

'No!'

She had some of the Mormons come round and watch me to make sure I didn't run off to the radio station.

I cried for weeks.

Trade never picked up at Jamie's salon, so I was doing much more housework and childminding and much less manicuring. In Brazil, you could retire after twenty-five years of working, and the quota of hours you put in during those years determined the amount of pension you were entitled to receive. Zylu was almost eligible to retire and she was putting in long hours to build up her quota and get the maximum amount of retirement money. That meant she could only come home once a month, so I was having to do everything in the house, and some manicuring as well. I didn't mind all that much because Jamie was easy to get along with and the children were in school most of the time.

Someone I knew through the salon was going to be travelling through Lageado and they asked if I wanted to send anything home. I was feeling bad about the letter I wrote my mother, even though it was never sent, and I felt I wanted to make it up to her. I had no money because I was paid so poorly, and the Mormons took ten percent of that. The rest I spent on some cheap clothes in case I ever happened to meet Rudolfo in the street. The Orlandini household did a monthly shop and I asked Jamie if I could send some food for my mother and pay him out of next month's wages.

'Take whatever you want, Rozana.'

'I'll replace it. Next month.'

'Whenever. Don't worry about it.'

I got a box and filled it up with supplies. I even sent a bar of milk chocolate. It was something my mother never had in her life and I smiled as I imagined her tasting it for the first time. How happy she would be when she opened the box! How impressed my brothers and sisters would be. They would never make fun of me again.

At the end of the month, my wages weren't enough to pay for what I'd sent, so I put some money away and, as Jamie said I could replace it whenever, I would rectify the balance the following month. This went on for a while and I never had quite enough to pay for the replacement supplies. Every time Zylu came home, she made sly remarks that stuff was missing from the cupboards. I wondered if Jamie told her I borrowed the supplies and she was hinting that I should put them back. Finally, she told me she wouldn't need my services any more as she was retiring in a couple of weeks.

'Please leave today and come back for your wages tomorrow.'

This took me completely by surprise because she always used to say I was her "gold" for looking after her "diamonds" so well, which is what she called her children.

'But I have nowhere to go, Zylu.'

'You should have thought of that before you stole the food.'

'I didn't steal it.'

'I gave you plenty of opportunities to put it back, but you didn't.'

'I was going to . . .'

'It's too late now, Rozana.'

I thought Jamie would back me up – explain what happened – but he just turned his head away. He wasn't prepared to go against his wife for a *camponese* like me.

I went round to the house of one of the other Mormons called Rosa and asked if I could stay there overnight.

'What happened with Zylu?'

'She let me go.'

'Why?'

'She doesn't need me anymore.'

Rosa was puzzled as to why Zylu would just put me out like that, but she agreed to let me stay without asking any more questions. Rosa's house was simple but comfortable. She was a nice woman of about forty and she was always looking in the mirror and saying "I only look thirty-five." In fact, she looked sixty.

The next day I went back to get my wages, but Zylu said she'd worked out the cost of the things I had taken from the house and I actually owed *her* money. She demanded I give her what I had saved to pay her back, and that left me with nothing. I couldn't believe she was treating me this way – a devout Christian who believed Jesus Christ was inside her, who cried in church and who called me her "gold." Why had she changed like this? Either her faith was fake – a facade – or something else had turned her heart to stone. I'd done nothing wrong, just borrowed some food for my hungry family, which I was going to replace. So why had I again become homeless with no money?

I started walking back towards Rosa's house, my head hanging and my back bent, as if I had been broken like a twig. I would have to beg Rosa to let me stay until I could find somewhere else, or ask her for the bus fare back to Lageado where everybody would laugh at me again and, like Zylu, believe I stole the supplies I sent home.

There was nothing else I could do – or was there?

The beginnings of a thought crossed my mind. I wouldn't have to take this kind of treatment from people if I worked for myself. If I was independent. I turned back from Rosa's house and went to see my friend Vera, the kindred spirit who was married to Carlos the butcher.

'Rozana, how lovely to see you!'

'Vera, I need a very big favour.'

'What is it?'

'Can you loan me thirty *reais* until tonight?'

'Of course.'

I was taking a big chance. There was no way I could know for sure that I'd be able to pay Vera back her money by the end of the day. It was a calculated risk. It was the first business decision I ever made and it was the first time I discovered the talent for enterprise that has got me to where I am today. Maybe it was inherent in me all along, like a seed waiting for the right conditions to sprout.

I went to a shop and bought a few bottles of nail polish and other small pieces of equipment, then I started knocking on people's doors, offering a mobile manicurist service.

There's something schizophrenic about the nature of the Brazilian psyche. They want to be better than the other person all the time, as they have a deep-rooted superiority complex and like to look down on lesser mortals. At the same time, they are always sympathetic to someone who needs help. Tell them a sad story and they'll cry. So, I told them my story – that I was homeless and desperately needed help. On the other hand, I was an excellent manicurist and could save them money and a trip to the salon. It was a formula that couldn't fail; a merger of Christian charity and simple economics.

By nightfall, I had made one hundred *reais* and most of the customers had booked a follow-up appointment. I went straight to Vera's and returned her thirty *reais*, then I went to Rosa's to get my things. It was 9:00pm, too late for the public toilets.

'I've spoken to my husband, Rozana.'

'Oh?'

'He said you can stay here if you help us with the rent.'

Perfect!

The next day I went knocking on doors again to get more clients. Within a few weeks, I was fully booked every day. It didn't mean I had lots of money. I didn't because I had to be cheaper and more convenient than the salons, but I was earning enough to pay my rent and buy food. I was a fifteen-year-old girl, living from day to day, moment to moment, trying to survive and not be ground down in the dirt.

I saw most other teenagers going round sporting the latest

fashions and I wanted to look like them. I wanted to live, not just exist. I had a couple of cheap dresses that I bought when I was with the Orlandinis, but I couldn't afford to buy new clothes. I worried in case I met Rudolfo. What would he think of me?

One of my door-to-door clients was a lady called Laura. She was blonde and pretty and she sold fashionable clothes from her house. Every time I went to do her nails, I would dream about wearing some of the wonderful garments she had in stock. One day I saw this beautiful blue top – it was heavenly! I touched it, felt it, smelled it and held it against my face. I wanted it so badly I could taste the longing. Laura had gone to get my money and, without thinking about it, I took off my own top and slipped on the blue one. Then I heard Laura coming back and I panicked. She would think I was trying to steal it and she'd tell everyone I was a thief. I'd lose all my clients. I didn't have time to get the top off and put my own back on, so I quickly pulled my top over the blue one.

The next time I went to do Laura's nails, I took the blue top with me in a bag. I was hoping to be able to put it back without her noticing. When she came to the door, she looked furious.

'Have you no shame?'

'What?'

'How could you even pass in front of my house?'

'I don't know what . . . '

'You stole from me, just like you did from Zylu!'

How did she know Zylu? It must have been through the Mormons. I tried to explain that it was a misunderstanding with Zylu, but she didn't want to listen.

'Did you take a top from this house?'

'It wasn't like that. I . . . '

'Did you or didn't you?'

I held up the bag.

'I brought it back.'

'Why, didn't it fit you?'

She grabbed the bag from my hand and looked inside.

'I'm telling everyone you're a thief. They won't let you inside their houses again.'

She slammed the door in my face.

My client base disintegrated overnight and I was back to square one.

Then Rosa's husband got promoted and the family had to move to São Paulo. They couldn't take me with them, but Rosa got me a job with one of her Mormon friends called Rachel Pereia.

Rachel was a middle-aged single mother with a nine-year-old son, Thiago. She ran a private language school that taught mainly English, but also Spanish and Italian. My job was to look after her son and do the cooking and cleaning.

The school was located in a big old American-style mansion near the city centre. Most of the rooms were used as classrooms and Rachel lived on the top floor in a big space that was a bedroom, kitchen and bathroom all in one. I had the everyday use of that room but slept on a mattress on the floor in one of the classrooms at night. Rachel and I got on well from the start. She liked me and I liked her. Although she was a Mormon, she didn't go to church for some reason, so I didn't go either.

Despite the school being exclusive, Rachel was finding it hard to manage financially because costs were so high in the city centre. The housework wasn't too taxing and Thiago was at school during the day, so she asked me to help out with the administration of the school. I was a quick learner and I found that I could be very versatile.

To begin with, I stood in for people who were off sick and, gradually, Rachel taught me about reception and customer service. She saw I could improvise and I was well organised, so she showed me how to read spreadsheets and balance sheets and do accounts and bookkeeping. I was fascinated. There was a whole new commercial world opening up before me. I became so efficient around the school she was able to cut back on admin staff and save on costs. She was really pleased with me.

I'd had breathing problems all my life and difficulty speaking without getting breathless. I don't know why. Maybe it was something to do with my poor diet, or the worms that crawled inside me when I was little. Rachel taught me to speak and breath properly and to walk with my head up and my back straight. She was always correcting my diction and commenting when I did something that was not within her sense of etiquette. To begin with, I thought she was picking on me.

'You never correct anyone else.'

'I don't care about them, Rozana. You're pretty and clever, but you could be much better.'

'Why do you care about me?'

'Because I believe you can do well in life.'

Every Friday, Rachel sent me and Thiago to her mother's house in the suburbs. We stayed there for the weekend and came back to the school on Monday. Her mother was a homely woman and very friendly. I called her "*avó*," just like Thiago did.

To try and repay Rachel for all she was doing for me, I had this great idea of offering free English courses to radio presenters in return for free advertising on their shows. It worked really well and, within a few months, the number of students had doubled. Rachel had to rent another house in the same street to accommodate the new classes. She also had to employ more teachers and a manager called Marcelo. I wanted to learn English too, as I spoke only Portuguese, but Rachel couldn't spare me as I was too busy with all my other work.

Marcelo was twenty-five and very handsome. He was extremely intelligent and read many psychological thriller books. I found him fascinating and, as he lived in one of the rooms at the new school, I began going there every weekend instead of to Rachel's mother's house with Thiago.

Marcelo was well travelled and he had many stories to tell about the places he'd been, the books he'd read and the people he'd met. We would sit at a little table and talk, sometimes all night. He told me to question things, to always ask *why*? He said I should never accept anything without knowing its true meaning. He opened little windows inside my head and let the light in, and I soared into the sky and knew what I was; what I could be.

His voice was soft and his words were like little kisses on my ears. He laughed at things other people didn't laugh at and thought about things the others didn't think about – things I didn't think about – until he made me. Then I thought about them all the time. He showed me things I hadn't seen before. Taught me things. How to listen. How to understand, just like I always imagined Rudolfo would do. I suppose I fell in love with him, but not in a romantic way like with Rudolfo. It was an intellectual love, pure and platonic. He paid a lot of attention to me and he made me feel special.

After a while, Rachel grew jealous of our relationship. It wasn't me with Marcelo she was jealous of, it was Marcelo with me. So, one Friday, she sent Thiago away to his grandmother's and said I could stay with her.

'You're nearly sixteen now, Rozana. I think you're mature enough.'

'Mature enough for what?'

'To learn a bit more about life.'

I was curious and wanted to know what it was I was going to learn. Maybe more about business practices?

'Be patient, Rozana.'

I was eager and looking forward to learning whatever it was.

In the evening, a couple about the same age as Rachel arrived. They were quite average, nothing exceptional about them, and I wondered who they were. Rachel served them wine and, shortly after, a younger couple arrived, along with two girls about my age. The girls looked poor, with cheap clothes and sad eyes. Rachel gave everyone a glass of wine, including me, but I didn't drink it because

I hated alcohol. One of the men looked at me.

'I see we have an observer tonight.'

Rachel smiled at him.

'She's a beginner.'

After a few glasses of wine, they started to get very friendly with each other – hugging and kissing and touching. I stood back, not wanting to get too close. Then Rachel suggested we all go upstairs to the bedroom. I was a bit scared at this stage, but curious about what was going on. This was a strange kind of business meeting and I still didn't know what I was supposed to learn. So I went with them.

Very soon, they were all naked and writhing round on the bed, all entwined with each other like a ball of worms. I kept looking – fascinated – as you can be by something that's unpleasant to look at, yet you cannot turn away. They didn't ask me to join in and I stayed well back against the wall – but I couldn't leave either, because Rachel had locked the door.

They stayed on the bed for about an hour, doing all sorts of things to each other. As I watched, I felt a mixture of disbelief and disgust, fascination and fear. When it was all over, they got dressed, drank some more wine and laughed and joked as if it was a respectable and polite social gathering. But when the others finally left, Rachel broke down in tears.

'I'm so sorry, Rozana. So sorry.'

'It's alright.'

'No, it's not.'

She kept apologising and saying she couldn't help it. Her voice was high-pitched and the words came quickly, hysterically. It was a compulsion, a high sex drive, hormones – she didn't know what. She hated that side of herself and it was why she stopped going to church. She had a chat room number for these people and she just rang it. Whoever came on the line, she invited round for sex.

'Isn't that dangerous, Rachel?'

'Of course it is, but I can't help it.'

I felt sorry for her, but good that she was confiding in me, and in a very personal way. It meant she trusted and valued me. It made me feel special, just like talking to Marcelo did.

As time passed, things began to get weirder. She had a special bidet in the toilet with a very strong jet. She began calling me in to watch her masturbate and I had to stay there until she had an orgasm. Then she began asking me to take my top off while I was watching her, wanting me to touch her. I always kept well back. It made me feel extremely embarrassed and uneasy and I wondered how long I could resist until she forced me to join in.

Why was this happening?

It seemed that every time things started to get better for me, something came along and fouled it all up. Was God laughing at me? Teasing me? Tormenting me for not keeping my promises? Was I destined to go through life like this, building my hopes and dreams, only to have them flung back in my face?

I had turned sixteen and I still had nothing to show for my life away from home. I felt empty, despite being in the company of these intelligent, educated people. They were teaching me things alright, some good and some bad, but I began to feel they were only using me to satisfy their own egos. I wasn't really *important* to them. They just liked to have me around because it made them feel special when they compared themselves to me.

I started to get depressed again and the blackness came over me, just as it had so many times before.

Like when I tried to kill myself.

I could see no way forward. I was trapped with these Mormons. I was drawn into their world and now there was no way out. I thought about ending my miserable life again – was close to doing it – searching for a way – putting it off in case things got better – but they didn't.

I fell deeper and deeper into depression, and the demon that had haunted me in the past came back to sit at the end of my bed and call to me in the night.

The final hurt came when Marcelo began to go out with one of the female teachers. She was blonde and pretty and nearer his age, so he had no time for me anymore. I was alright when he came first and didn't know anyone, but she started being with him all the time, which meant I couldn't go there on weekends. I either had to accompany Thiago or stay with Rachel and put up with her perversions. I couldn't bear it anymore, so I told Rachel I wanted to go home. She said it was a mistake and tried to talk me out of it, but I knew if I didn't go back to Lageado – I would go to hell.

CHAPTER NINE
THE CURANDEIRO

It was a long bus journey home, through the night. I brought a little blanket with me, as it was always colder in the south. All the people on the bus looked ugly, particularly the man who sat next to me. He was about fifty, he had no teeth and he smelled of something unidentifiable. I fell asleep for a while and eventually woke again, feeling cold. I looked across and he was covered with my blanket. I took the blanket back, but this happened again. I pushed him when I took it back the second time, intending it to be a warning. He obviously took it the wrong way because, next time I woke, his hands were under the blanket with me, touching me. I was disgusted, so I went and told the driver, who stopped the bus and moved the man away from me. But he kept looking back, grinning his toothless grin, and I was unable to sleep for the rest of the night.

My mother was surprised to see me back so soon after sending her the food parcel. She believed I had finally been able to make something of myself judging by the quality of provisions I'd recently sent, yet I was home again, with my head down and my back bent.

'What happened this time?'

'I can't tell you.'

'Why not?'

'I just can't.'

My mother didn't ask any more questions. She was a very stoical woman and took everything life threw at her in her stride. Worse things had happened to her. She watched two of her children die in her arms, so me being home again was a just a minor disappointment.

For the first time in many years, all her surviving children were at home together – my brothers Antonio, José, Manoel and Dirceu – my sisters Nicole, Celia and Dirce – and me. The little house was crowded. It was a joy for her in one way, and a hardship in another. The motorway had reached Lageado and it had brought more Germans who were clearing the forests and establishing farms and plantations, so work was becoming more available and wages were improving. The Germans paid a higher hourly rate than local landowners, which forced the Brazilians to improve working conditions as well. My brothers were building their own houses and my sisters were forming relationships. They would be leaving the family hut one day and there would be nobody left but my mother, my father and Antonio – and me.

I was a failure.

Good for nothing.

I had tried several times to make a better life for myself, but each time God had intervened and drove me back home. It was my fate for the things I did with Daniel when I was so very young; what I allowed him to do to me.

I became a joke to my brothers and sisters. My mother had shown them the supplies I sent her, boasted to them about my good life in Maringá, shared the milk chocolate with them. They were impressed and envious. Rozana, the most insignificant of the pack when growing up, was now the most important.

Then I came home. Head down. Back bent. Beaten. They laughed at me and ridiculed me and their jibes were like the lashes of whips, cutting into my bare flesh.

'So how much money have you made, Rozana?'

'Did you bring any of those magazines? You know, the ones with your pictures on the cover?'

'When is Rudolfo coming to meet the family?'

'You almost arrived back before the food you sent!'

'Did you steal it?'

I couldn't bring myself answer them, because they were right. It was my destiny to live in Lageado for the rest of my life – to work on a farm and marry a *pobre operário* who would make me have many children for him, beat me when he got drunk and blame me for keeping him poor. That's if anyone would have me after the scandal of seducing Paulo Oliviera.

I would probably end up old and alone, stealing from my neighbours to stay alive and accepting the poverty that was going to be part of the rest of my life. I would never see the places Marcelo told me about, never read the books, never meet the people, never understand the meaning of this life, apart from the endless treadmill of trying to survive.

The first thing I had to do was get a job. So I went with my mother to work on a plantation owned by Joao, the eldest brother of Ramon and Daniel. He gave me a job digging weeds from a huge soya field. Working ten hours a day, it would take me three weeks to complete the job and I wouldn't get paid until I finished. I suppose I could have went to the Germans, but it didn't work out with them the last time, so I was resigned to know my place and stick with my own kind. It was a two hour walk to the plantation and, on that first morning, I saw Daniel coming towards me as I traipsed along with my mother. I was sixteen – ten years older than when he'd abused me – but the shame was still in me and I kept my head down while he passed.

He did the same.

It was November and already the temperature was climbing to thirty-five degrees celsius during the day. The field was about ten acres in size and I was alone in it. The weeds were waist-high and I had a weeding hoe called an *enchada* to dig them out before piling them by the side of the field to rot. There was always the danger of snake bites, some of which were poisonous, like the coral snake or the viper, and I had to be careful where I stepped. My mother worked elsewhere on the plantation and she would come and collect me every evening.

To begin with, I imagined if I worked hard I might be able to save some money and get my own small plot of land – grow my own crops and get a cow and build a little hut in a cherry tree. Ramon was dead, but maybe I could achieve our childhood dream alone. Then I wouldn't need a man to marry me and make me carry his children and beat me and then blame me. But it was just a dream, like it always had been. After two weeks of working in the heat and the rain, without enough food to eat, reality set in. It would never happen. It was just too hard.

I began to feel very tired and depressed again.

One day it got so hot I felt like I was going to pass out. There was a small river close to the soya field, so I went down there to drink some water and wash my face and neck. When I stood up to go back to work, my legs wouldn't respond. There was no one else about and I staggered back to the field, holding onto whatever I could for support. I collapsed amongst the weeds and soya plants and lay there out of sight of anyone who might be passing. At the end of the day, my mother came to look for me. She couldn't see me at first and I could hear her calling.

'Rozana! Rozana!'

By then I had started to hallucinate. A red rash appeared all over my body and my stomach felt like it was on fire. I heard my mother's voice but wasn't sure if it was real. I tried to call back.

'Mãe . . . mãe . . . '

She came and found me. A look of shock came over her face when she saw the state I was in.

'What happened? Were you bitten?'

'No.'

'What did you do?'

'I drank the water.'

I pointed towards the river.

'That water is contaminated with chemicals from weed and

insect killers!'

My mother left me lying in the soya field. I raised my arms to her, for her to take me with her. I thought she was leaving me there to die because I was such a disappointment to her – to die all alone, at the mercy of the ghosts and Ramon's great-grandmother. Everything was starting to grow dim and I thought night was falling. Then my mother re-appeared, leading a horse she borrowed from the landowner. She helped me up onto its back and I clung on for the two-hour trudge home.

When we got there, my mother tried to make me better with camomile and fennel flowers. She even rubbed sugar into my legs like she used to do to stop the worms coming up and out of my mouth. But nothing worked. I just got sicker and sicker. Everyone believed I was going to die. I was in constant excruciating pain and it felt like there was a steel band round my stomach and it was getting tighter and tighter. I threw anything I tried to eat back up and my vital organs were beginning to shut down.

Death was drawing near.

People started coming to the hut to pay their last respects.

Then a woman called Nair came and told my mother she knew of a man who could cure anything. I would have to be taken to him and he lived in the middle of the forest. My mother borrowed the horse again. This time she had to tie me onto its back to prevent me from falling, because I was too weak to hold on.

She and Nair set off across the farmland and fields with me, until we came to the edge of the forest. There was no track or trail to follow and Nair only had a vague idea of where the man lived, so we trekked through rough terrain, making very slow progress for several hours.

Finally, after what seemed like eternity, we emerged into a clearing with a big old ramshackle house that had beautiful wild flowers growing all around it and a clear sparkling spring running close by. I was only half aware of what was happening, but I could see Nair going up to the door while my mother held the horse. A very old man with long white hair came out. He had dark skin and a white beard and he looked very fragile – almost as fragile as me. Nair spoke to him for a short while, but I couldn't hear what they were saying.

His name was Aroldo. He came over and took me from the horse and carried me into the house. I had lost so much weight that I was no heavier than a little doll and could easily be carried, even by an old man like him.

The house was bare inside, with no furniture, except for a single wooden table. It had an earth floor, like our hut, and a big brick fireplace. Many jars hung from nails in the walls, containing all sorts of concoctions. There was a hammock where he slept and an old guitar which he played for his own pleasure and no one else's. Aroldo was a *Curandeiro* – a Shaman, or Witchdoctor in English – a faith healer who could cure with natural remedies and by using the mysterious forces of spirits and ghosts.

He put me on the table and looked inside my mouth, then he pressed hard on my stomach. It hurt so much that it made me cry.

'Poison.'

My mother was amazed how he knew straight away what was wrong with me.

'How can you tell?'

'By her mouth.'

He disappeared for a long time, maybe half an hour. I feared he wouldn't come back. Perhaps he knew he couldn't cure me and I was going to die. Thankfully, he did return, carrying a big tin with a lot of green stuff inside. He put fire to the mixture and a big flame shot out of it. He blew the smoke into my face and began walking around me, chanting over me and clicking his fingers. I couldn't understand the words he was reciting. They were alien to me – not Portuguese or any other language I had heard. When he was finished, he gave my mother one of his jars with a dark green liquid and leaves inside it.

'She must take it all, leaves as well.'

My mother thanked him and offered him money, which he refused to take. He then carried me outside and put me back on the horse.

As soon as we got home, I began to take the medicine. It was horrible – very bitter – and the taste stayed in my mouth for hours, but it did at least stay down. I took the potion every morning until it was all gone. It lasted about a week and the bitter taste remained on my tongue the whole time. Miraculously, I was already feeling better by the time I had finished it and my father got some bananas, which I managed to eat. It was the first food I'd taken in several weeks without being sick.

The next day, I managed to go outside without help and no one could believe it. They thought I had died and this was my spirit leaving my body. They ran away and hid in their houses and I thought to myself: *Nothing will ever change here. They will always be superstitious and ignorant, and I will never get used to it.*

I smiled with one side of my face and scowled with the other.

I owed my life to the *Curandeiro* and I wanted to thank him personally. I knew he wouldn't accept any kind of reward, so I took him one of my poems. I travelled into the forest and tried to retrace the way we came when I was sick. As I was quite literally dying then, I couldn't remember the route at all and I seemed to be going round in circles for hours. Then I heard a sound, unlike any of the forest noises. I listened intently and heard it again. It was a musical note, played on a guitar string. Not a melody or a tune of any sort, just a single note. It sounded again and I followed it, trying to fathom its symmetry; its meaning. It seemed to be calling me – luring me – into its strange enchanted essence. I emerged into the clearing with the big old house, surrounded by wild flowers.

Everything was still and quiet.

Otherworldly.

Eternal.

Time seemed to be standing still there in the clearing. I approached the house and called the *Curandeiro's* name.

'Aroldo.'

There was no reply, so I tested the door, which was unlocked. I opened it and looked inside.

'Aroldo . . . '

He wasn't home, but the old guitar was there, lying close to the hammock. I went back outside and sat down and waited. After about an hour, Aroldo came back. He was carrying a bag full of leaves, berries, herbs and flowers. He didn't seem at all surprised to see me.

'Ah, the poisoned girl. How did you get here?'

'I heard you playing.'

'Playing?'

'The guitar.'

'Ahh . . . '

He smiled wryly and put down his sack. Then he sat beside me on the ground.

'I've come to thank you.'

'For what?'

'For saving my life.'

'I did not save your life.'

'But . . . '

'You were not meant to die.'

He took a bottle from his pocket and offered it to me. I hesitated, looking carefully at the clear liquid inside. He laughed.

'It's water, from the spring.'

I drank the water and gave him my poem.

'What is this?'

'A poem. For you. To thank you.'

'I cannot read.'

And so I read it to him.

The wind blows hard, the sky is scarred
My soul stands still, upon the hill
It looks away, its dead eyes stray
To floating clouds, like ghostly shrouds

I watch it there, wind blows my hair
I hear my name, called through a flame
I turn around, drink the compound
Aroldo's smile ends my harsh trial

I walk towards him and leave the brim
Of the dark hill. We meet, stand still
He turns the tide of tears I cried
And lets me live, my thanks I give

The wind has gone and I walk on
The clouds have blown away and flown
The sky is blue, the world is new
My soul and I, our hopes soar high

It was just a simple verse, originally meant for a lover I never had. But I re-wrote some of the words to make it fit the situation. When I finished, he took the poem from me and placed the paper to his forehead. He held it there for a long time, his eyes closed. Then he spoke in a voice that seemed to be coming, not from his mouth, but from the forest all around us.

'Rozana . . . '

He knew my name.

'You do not belong here.'

'Where?'

'In Lageado.'

'Where *do* I belong?'

'In your own world. In your own time.'

'How do I get there?'

'You are already there.'

Then he went inside the house, taking the poem with him, and closed the door.

I waited for a while to see if he would come back out. When he did not, I left and made my way back through the forest. I heard the note again, the musical note, away in the distance. Saying goodbye. And I knew what I had to do.

When I got a bit stronger, I went back to finish the job on the plantation. I felt renewed when it was done and I stood in the middle of the soya field that was finally free of weeds. I felt ready to take on the world again. I knew I could do it. The *Curandeiro* told me I could.

When I went to see Joao to get paid, he said he didn't have all my money. He offered me vouchers to spend in the plantation shop. Farmers were like that, always complaining they had no money. They would give you vouchers to keep you there. You spent the vouchers in their shops and they owned you.

But not me. I wanted cash.

'I can give you half now and half in three weeks time.'

'I want it all.'

'It's the best I can do.'

So I had to settle for half, because I knew I couldn't stay for three weeks to collect the rest. I had to go right then, or I wouldn't go at all.

My mother was working, so I left her a note–

Dear Mãe,
I have to go away again. This time I will not come back
until I have made something of myself. I am going back
to the city and you will not hear from me again until
I have done what I need to do.

Do not worry about me. I will make you proud. Also,
Joao only paid me half the money he owes me. You
can have the rest.
Your loving daughter,
Rozana

Even though the bus stop was closer because of the motorway, it took me longer than usual to walk there. A concrete path had been laid and it got very hot in the midsummer sun, blistering my bare feet. I had to keep stopping to cool them. While I was walking, I decided what I would do. I would go back to Rachel in Maringá and put up with her sexual perversion for a while until I built up my manicure business again. I knew she'd be glad to see me because she didn't want me to leave in the first place. I would say to Rachel: "I'm sorry, I made a mistake." She'd say she told me so, but not to worry about it because she missed me.

In the meantime, I would also go see some of the radio presenters who got free English lessons from my scheme and maybe get my arts show back, maybe even one that paid a salary.

On the bus journey back, I hoped I wouldn't see the toothless guy who tried to sexually assault me on the way down. I got a seat near the back with nobody beside me. However, the bus was packed and there were two more passengers to get on – one was a huge woman and the other was a really good-looking boy. One of them was bound to sit next to me. The big woman got on first and made her way straight to where I was sitting. *Just my luck*! I thought, as I was squeezed up against the window by the size of her hips. There was only one other seat left, and that was a window seat behind us. The youth made his way down the bus and when he came to the big woman, he smiled at her.

'I hurt my leg in a motorbike accident. I need to have an aisle seat.'

She couldn't resist his smile and she moved to the other seat, letting him sit next to me. During the night, it started to rain and I couldn't close the window. I was getting wet, even with the blanket over me.

'Sit closer to me.'

He moved his arm so I could get right in to him.

'That way, you won't get wet.'

His arm went around me as I snuggled up to him. It was better than being next to the old toothless guy and I felt strangely safe.

I finally fell asleep on the bus, thinking about my plans, and only woke up when the driver shook me.

'We're in Maringá, miss.'

It was 6:00am. The good-looking boy was gone and I didn't get the chance to thank him for his consideration – or get his phone number. I went straight to Rachel's house but all the lights were off, so I waited outside. I didn't want to disturb anyone too early. After about an hour, a light came on upstairs, so I went to the door and knocked, with a big expectant smile on my face. Thiago opened it. When he saw me, his mouth twisted into a hostile grimace.

'What are you doing here, thief?'

I was shocked. I had always got on well with the boy before. Obviously, the Mormons had been spreading their hate lies, even to Rachel. My smile faded.

'What are you talking about, Thiago?'

'You stole from Zylu, and from Laura.'

'Wait a minute . . . '

'And you stole a Hard Rock T-shirt from me.'

'I did not!'

'Yes you did!'

I don't know why he accused me of that. Maybe he just mislaid the T-shirt and assumed I took it because he heard all the grownups saying I stole things. I could hear Rachel's voice calling down from the bedroom.

'Who is it?'

'It's the thief, mama.'

I left before she came down. I didn't want to have to explain myself to her. If they wanted to believe I was a thief, I wouldn't try to convince them otherwise.

Once more, my careful plans had all gone awry. I didn't know what to do. I certainly couldn't go home *again* – especially after leaving that note for my mother. Then I heard the musical note of the old *Curandeiro's* guitar echoing in my head. I put my hand into my pocket and pulled out the money I had left, to check exactly how much. A small piece of paper came out with it – a phone number. I tried to think of whose it was.

Then I remembered.

George, the Brazilian Elder who prepared me for entering into the Mormon church gave it to me. He said if I was ever in São Paulo I should give him a call. It was a sign! I *had* to go to São Paulo.

It was beginning to get dark by the time the bus pulled out of Maringá, and I had just enough money for the fare, with a little change left over. São Paulo was a long way from Lageado.

There would be no going back.

Not this time.

CHAPTER TEN
SÃO PAULO

I arrived in São Paulo at 6:30am on Saturday 23rd December 1989. I was just two months away from turning seventeen. I got off the bus in a huge station called Tiete, with coaches coming from all over Brazil, as well as Bolivia, Paraguay, Uruguay and numerous other parts of South America. It was a maelstrom of sound and movement and it filled me with awe. I didn't know what to do, so I just followed the other people who got off with me. They seemed to know where they were going, but soon they all dispersed and I was left alone in the middle of millions.

I was overwhelmed by the size of everything – the sheerness of the sights, the sounds and the smells, the noise of traffic, the thickness of the air and the movement coming from all around me. I had never seen anything like this. I was frightened and excited at the same time.

São Paulo was in full Christmas swing, with all the shop windows decorated and sandwich-board *Papai Noels* ringing bells in the sweltering sun. There were street traders peddling food, plastic toys, cheap cigarettes and counterfeit branded goods from stalls and boxes. Hundreds of people going in different directions – all in a hurry, trying to outpace each other and ignore each other at the same time. The shrill, screaming noise of police and ambulance sirens. Impatient drivers hooting their horns and shouting and swearing at each other in an impossible gridlock. Local buses with people hanging off the doors and windows and crowding on top of the roofs. Emaciated stray dogs with mange and ticks and fleas and flies everywhere and people sleeping on the pavement, with the scurrying throng tripping over them.

The sounds filled my senses and the smells of the food mingled with the stench of sewage from a distant canal or some peripheral river and the faint, smoky odour of urine drifted on the midsummer air. It was a new world, full of nervous energy and garish colours – and I thought I would sink down into the sordid wonder of it all, never to be seen again.

I sat on a bench, just observing the constant ebb and flow around me. What had I done? How could I survive here, where I knew nobody and nobody knew me – much less cared about me? I looked at the ragged beggars and wondered if they, like me, had come to this place in search of a new life.

I was so hungry I felt weak, like I was going to pass out. All I'd had to eat the previous day was one slice of bread and the initial adrenaline rush of arriving in this city soon gave way to the realities of life in São Paolo. All I had left was a few *centavos* and that was not enough to buy anything. The temptation to grab some food from a street vendor and make a run for it was overpowering, but what if I was caught? The police carried sticks and guns – they would beat me or shoot me. So I discarded the idea and wandered around for a while, trying to find a public telephone, until I came to a metro station. People were heading down there so maybe I should too?

I had never been under ground before – so far underground. It was amazing. Unnatural. The air was recycled and had been used so many times it had lost its vitality. It tasted dusty, dry, dishevelled. People had tickets to get them through the barriers. I did not, but I was small enough to duck underneath. On the platform, frantic crowds were pushing and crushing and I worried that some of them would fall onto the tracks – but they managed to balance on the edge without going over it. It was rush-hour and the trains were so packed it was difficult for the doors to close. The heat and humidity were almost unbearable and I kept well back against the wall until the morning madness was over.

Then I got on a train.

I got off at the next station and got back on the following train. I did this at every stop, just to practise getting on and off without getting caught in the closing doors. I had no idea where I was going, until I came to a station called "República." I liked the name, so I got off and followed the people to the surface, ducking under the barrier again on the way out into the freshness and natural light. República station was huge, just like Tiete bus terminal. It had escalators, clothes stalls, food outlets and a big square called Praça da República outside, with trees and a fountain. I checked the piece of paper with Elder George's number and searched for a public phone again. I found one that resembled a giant ear, but it was different to the phones in Maringá and other places I had been and I wasn't sure how to use it correctly. I had to buy a special coin called a *ficha* to make the call – a *ficha* cost twenty *centavos* and I had thirty-two.

I would only have one chance.

I made a few practice attempts, without putting any money in, but I couldn't get it right. I was scared and overawed and intimidated by the enormity of the task I had taken on by going to São Paulo. I felt so small and insignificant. So useless. Ill-equipped for whatever lay ahead of me. I started to cry. A man came over.

'What's the matter?'

'I don't know how to use the phone.'

'Who do you want to call?'

I gave him the piece of paper and twenty *centavos* and he made the call for me. He handed me the phone with a smile and walked away. I listened to the ringing tone at the other end. Then a man's voice answered.

'Hello.'

'George?'

'George is not here right now.'

'Who are you?'

'I'm George's father. Who are you?'

'I'm Rozana Ramos, George's friend. He told me to call him if I came to São Paulo.'

'Where are you now?'

'At a metro station. República.'

Then the money ran out and the line went dead.

'Hello! Hello! Hello!'

It was no use. The call was over and I didn't have enough money to make another. Tears ran down my face. They were warm and salty when they reached my lips and I was so hungry they even tasted good.

Time passed slowly, sighing in my ear. I had been lonely many times in the past – very lonely and forsaken at times, but the kind of loneliness I felt now was different. It was total. A forlornness I had never experienced before. A hopelessness so dark and deep it enveloped me in its disconsolate shroud. Perhaps the best thing I could do would be to go back down into the metro and throw myself under a train. I was so lost in my despair that I didn't notice a man in his fifties – wearing a white shirt and dark trousers – approaching me. He touched my shoulder, making me jump.

'Don't be afraid.'

'Who are you?'

'You called me.'

'George's father?'

'Yes. I'm Tony. And you are Rozana?'

I don't know how he managed to recognise me in the midst of all those people. Maybe I looked as lost as I felt, like a scrawny stray cat. He asked what time I arrived and how I got to the station. He was amazed that I'd managed to negotiate the metro alone without ever being on it before.

'Are you hungry?'

'Yes.'

He bought me some *pão de queijo*, which was a kind of local cheese bread, from a takeaway outlet. I devoured it in seconds. Then he paid for tickets and took me back down into the asthmatic air of the metro. We travelled five or six stops, changing trains a couple of times, before getting off at a station called Trianon-Masp. We caught a local bus with standing room only and, after a couple of hours of being stuck in the gridlocked traffic, we arrived at a suburb called Campo Limpo.

Tony had a small ground-floor flat in a large block surrounded by other high-rise apartments. He lived there with his wife and seventeen-year-old daughter. George wasn't there because he was away on a mission. The family were nice people and they wanted to know how I met George, who they were obviously very proud of. They were Mormons too and Tony was the leader of a local church. The flat was small and Tony said I would not be able to stay there for very long.

'Are you a Mormon, Rozana?'

'Yes.'

It wasn't a lie. I had been initiated into their church.

'Then tomorrow I'll ask the members to help you.'

The next day was Sunday, and Christmas Eve, and we all went to church together. The Mormons always celebrated Christmas on the Sunday before Christmas Day and the church was adorned with red and green decorations – peppertree branches with green leaves and red berries and wreaths of wild poinsettia. The sermon was all about the birth of Jesus and the choir sang their own Mormon carols. Afterwards there was food and drink, but I was very reserved at first. My previous experiences with the Mormons were not good and I was finding it difficult to interact with those people. Then I saw a familiar face in the crowd. It was Rosa, the woman who took me in when Zylu threw me out and who introduced me to Rachel Pereia, before moving to São Paulo. She saw me too and came over.

'Rozana, how lovely to see you.'

'It's great to see you too, Rosa.'

'How long have you been in São Paulo?'

'I arrived yesterday.'

She asked if I had a job and somewhere to live and I said neither, but Tony Araújo was kind enough to put me up temporarily.

'You must come live with me. I will find you a job. Life in São Paulo isn't easy and we can help each other with the bills. It will be just like Maringá again.'

And so it was arranged. Rosa came to Tony's flat with me after church and we collected my things. We walked down the long straight road to her house. It took about an hour and the further we travelled, the poorer, more rundown and violent-looking the areas became. Eventually, we crossed a little bridge over a canal. It was stagnant and stank in the summer heat, clogged with rubbish and old discarded furniture.

Rosa's house was in the middle of a large slum – a *curtiço* in a place called Vila Sonia. The slum was much larger than the one in Maringá where I lived with Samuel's mother-in-law, and Rosa's house was close to the canal – just three or four meters away. The houses there were makeshift and made of brick and sand, but with no concrete, so when it rained and the level of the canal rose, some of them got swept away. Further down the street, the *curtiço* was poorer and more dilapidated and the houses were *favella*-like and made of cardboard. Rosa told me drug dealers operated openly in the narrow back-alleys and a vegetable seller was shot dead there recently. There were no proper streets, just earthen roads, and no rubbish collection, so everything got dumped into the canal. The sewage also got pumped into the canal and that's why it stank to high heaven in the summer heat.

All the people in Vila Sonia worked, but wages were low and the cost of living was high, so they could not afford proper housing. Rosa's house had one bedroom, a small kitchen with a basic cooker and a little sink. The shower-toilet was shared with three other households. There were two beds, one for Rosa and her husband

and the other for her two children – a boy aged five and a girl aged eleven. I slept on the floor in the kitchen.

I expected the house to be much better as they left Maringá because her bus-driver husband got promoted. But although he was earning more money, the cost of living there was ten times higher, so they were actually worse off. I didn't say anything because it would have sounded ungrateful, but secretly I wished I had stayed with Tony and his family.

There were two kinds of poverty in Brazil – rural poverty, with hunger, backwardness and no amenities like shops, showers or television – and urban poverty, with squalor, filth and disease.

Urban poverty was worse.

Although Rosa was a Mormon, she still celebrated Christmas Day in the traditional Brazilian Catholic way, with dinner at midnight on Christmas Eve. The food was traditional – roast pork leg and rice with apricots and raisins – and I was starving. Rosa was unemployed and she said we could go together to the city centre on Tuesday, when the Christmas holiday was over, to look for jobs. I had intended to go knocking on doors, like I did before, but she said it would be easier just to buy a newspaper.

She woke me early on the Tuesday, around 5:00am, and we took a bus to Central São Paulo. The journey was surreal for me. Tall buildings like rectangular mountains surrounded the bus and the streets were thronged with vehicles of all shapes and sizes, even at that early hour. The people looked so impassive, as if they were not human at all, but alien beings from another planet. Automatons. Emotionless. Rosa saw my apprehension. She smiled and held my hand.

'You'll get used to all this.'

'Will I?'

We bought a newspaper in a newsagents and stood there going through the job ads. I found one for a manicurist in a salon on *Av Ipiranga*.

'That's not far from here, Rozana.'

'Let's go there.'

We walked a few blocks and entered a huge building called the Edifício Copan, with a plaque saying it was designed by Oscar Niemeyer, the most famous Brazilian architect who ever lived. In the ground-floor gallery, I saw a narrow door with the name "Terezanet."

'That's the place, Rosa.'

'Go on then. I'll wait out here for you.'

I took a deep breath and went in. There were no other applicants – maybe I had a chance.

'I've come to apply for the manicurist job.'

I showed the newspaper ad to the lady in reception.

'Take a seat, please.'

After a few minutes, the manager came and took me to into the salon to do a test. There were about a dozen other girls working there – manicurists and hairdressers and beauticians. The manager selected a girl and told me to do her nails. I was really nervous and my hands were shaking. One of the hairdressers approached me. Her voice was soft and reassuring.

'My name is Malu. What's yours?'

'Rozana.'

'Don't be nervous, Rozana. It'll be alright.'

When I finished, all the girls who worked there came to look at the job I had done. I could tell by their expressions that they were not impressed. The manager turned to Malu, who was a supervisor.

'What do you think?'

'I think it's very good.'

He asked me a few questions – how old I was, what my previous experience was, where I lived and would I be able to get there on time in the mornings. *Yes I would*! He gave me a list of documents to bring with me – ID, CIC and registration.

'Pay is commission only, and tips. Is that alright?'

'Yes.'

'Can you start tomorrow?'

'Yes.'

'Seven o'clock.'

Malu waved to me on the way out and smiled.

'See you tomorrow, Rozana.'

I found it hard to get to sleep that night. I was anxious about working in such a big salon and how I would fit in, as well as how early I would have to get up to be there by seven. I tossed and turned on my mattress on the kitchen floor, getting more worried about being late for my first day in my new job with every hour that went by. I think maybe I got about two hours sleep before leaving Rosa's house at 4:00am. I had to walk for half an hour to get to the bus stop. It was still dark, with no street lights and most of the houses had their lights off, too. I walked quickly, scared by every shadow and every sound, looking over my shoulder as I scurried along. By the time I arrived at the bus stop, the queue was already quite lengthy and I couldn't get a seat. Every time we stopped, there was a scrum of people trying to get a space on a bus that was already full.

By the time we got to the city centre, people were hanging onto the outside and we were packed like sardines on the inside. I was so worried about not being able to get out in time, I fought my way to the door too early and got off at the wrong stop. I didn't know where I was and had to ask for directions from a few people. After a long walk, I finally arrived at Edifício Copan. It was 6:45am. Malu was already in the salon, which made me feel at ease. She showed me round and introduced me to the others and told me to make myself a cup of coffee.

My shift was from 7:00am to 7:00pm. Most of the clients who came in had their own preferred manicurist, so it was a very long day for me, sitting there doing nothing and worrying if I was ever going to make any commission. I had borrowed the bus fare from Rosa and I had no money for food and only one slice of bread to eat before I left that morning. Malu tried to make life easier for me by talking to me when she wasn't busy and telling the clients that the salon had a new manicurist they should try. Unfortunately, very few followed her advice. Malu was a genuinely nice person and I probably would not have stayed, but for her.

It was 10:00pm by the time I got back to Rosa's house that evening. The journey was just as scary as in the morning and I almost ran the whole way from the bus stop. There was no dinner ready for me and no food in the house. Rosa and her husband both worked shifts – him on the busses, and she got herself a job at McDonalds. Sometimes they would be there when I got in and sometimes they would not.

The routine was the same every day for the first week.

I found it hard going – sleeping three hours, walking in the dark in a dangerous area, crammed onto the bus for hours, very little food, boring conditions in the salon and no commission. But slowly the clients warmed to me and I made friends with some of the other salon girls. I became particularly close to Adelena, who was a blonde, fifty-year-old masseuse. She had a daughter a little older than me who she didn't get on with, so she called me *"filha,"* which is Portuguese for daughter. That's just how she treated me. She would share her packed lunch with me, saying she was on a diet. I found out afterwards she wasn't on a diet at all, but packed extra food for me.

Malu continued to do everything she could to help and encourage me and she got me credit in a local café until I got paid. I couldn't just keep taking Adelena's food. But the days were still long – from leaving Rosa's house at 4:00am until getting back there at 10:30pm. I had to keep borrowing the bus fare from Rosa until I got my first monthly pay, so when I did get the small pittance I had earned, I owed it all and there was nothing left. So I had to start borrowing and getting credit and taking free food all over again, until the next payday.

It was a vicious circle.

There was a television comedy show in Brazil at the time called *A Praça é Nossa*, and they were looking for extras to be on set. I thought this might be a good way to break into the entertainment business. The wages had to be better than what I was earning and the work would surely be more interesting. Auditions were being held in Tietê, which is a town about seventy miles or so to the north west of Sâo Paulo. The bus fare to get there was expensive, almost a week's wages, and I had no resume or experience. Still, I decided to give it a try.

When I got to the audition venue, I checked in at reception and the girl there told me I was expected to bring my own makeup. I had no makeup, so I went out into the streets to see what I could find to improvise with. There was a hardware depot about half a mile away and I found some charcoal there, which I used for eye-liner. On the way back, it started to rain and the charcoal ran down my cheeks. I looked like a clown. They were taking pictures of people at the auditions when I got back. They took a photo of me with my *palhaço* face and told me to leave a number.

They never called.

The weeks rolled by and despite the long hours and a greater number of clients, I still wasn't earning much money. After rent and travel fares and food, there was very little left over. The initial loneliness I felt in República station never really left me and, gradually, I became very depressed – clinically depressed. I didn't know I was clinically depressed, because I'd never heard of clinical depression, or unipolar disorder, or MDD. I just knew that, sometimes, when I went up the thirty-eight floors onto the roof of Edifício Copan, I felt like jumping off, like others had done before me. The only thing that stopped me was the note I left for my mother, promising I would make her proud. She had suffered all her life and I could not give her more pain.

The sadness I felt inside was like being possessed by some entity other than myself. The forlorn shroud of hopelessness enveloped me all the time and I could not shake it off. Sometimes I wished I'd never been born. I felt physically ill. The muscles in my face felt stiff and a heavy lump was lodged inside my chest. I couldn't see any point in getting up in the morning; in carrying on.

But I did.

I never missed a single day's work, despite the way I felt – but I would attend to the clients without ever looking up to see who they were. It wasn't important who they were. They weren't people to me – just numerous feet. My life consisted of nothing but cleaning feet.

Was this the future the old *Curandeiro* foresaw for me?

CHAPTER ELEVEN
ARRESTED

As time went by my depression deepened and I suffered in resigned silence. Malu was more like an older sister to me than a supervisor. All the other girls in the salon were too busy with their work and their lives to pay any attention to me, but Malu knew something was wrong. She could tell I had changed. It was more than just feeling unhappy – it was a kind of hopelessness.

When I was younger, I thought of depression as a form of attention-seeking and an obsession with my large breasts. All I saw in the mirror were two big ugly boobs that made me look like a grotesque beast, but that was my imagination playing tricks. What I saw in the mirror was not reality, but something my mind conjured up.

This was different.

Darker.

I was telling myself I didn't deserve to be happy. I was worthless – life was worthless. No one would care if I died. There was no point in living. There was no way out of the darkness, no matter what I did, so there was no point in doing anything. I was overcome by feelings of listlessness and inertia – and bitterness. Everyone around me was stupid and horrible and I couldn't see goodness or beauty in anything.

Malu suggested that maybe I should move closer to my job. Getting up so early and having to travel so far was probably affecting my mood. If I lived closer to the salon, I wouldn't be so tired all the time and that might help. She showed me how to look for accommodation and we found a room in a shared house that was only a ten-minute walk away.

Rosa was upset at my leaving. She said if I got myself into trouble, I wasn't welcome back. I was sorry to have upset her after she'd been kind enough to take me in. She depended on the money I paid her and life would be more difficult after I left. But I had to put my mental health before anything else and if that meant moving, then so be it.

It was a big old three-story house in an area of the city centre called Bexiga. The house was owned by a man called Carlo and he had divided it up into singles accommodation. There were at least a dozen people living there at any one time, with tenants coming and going regularly. My room was on the ground floor. It had two bunk beds and one single bed and I shared with two other girls. There was a shower/toilet on each floor and one massive kitchen on the ground floor that was shared by the whole house. We all bought our own food, though I rarely cooked there, and I usually went straight to my bed when I got in from work. All the tenants were single working people and I didn't get too close to any of them, even the girls I was sharing a room with. Carlo lived in the house and when the lights went out at 10:00pm he would go round each room to make sure everyone was in bed. If you were late, you had to find your way in the dark. It was like living in the dormitory of a boarding school.

The shared house was a crazy place. During the time I lived there, I saw more people coming and going than in my whole life up to then. The house was in a street where prostitutes stood all night looking for clients, so Carlo always left some rooms empty that could be rented to the hookers on an hourly basis. I worked at least twelve hours a day, six days a week, so I really only went back there to sleep and only mixed with the other tenants in the kitchen on Sundays. One night, I was woken by a commotion upstairs. People were running round and shouting and police sirens were shrieking outside. I got out of bed to see what was going on and was told that a prostitute had been killed in one of the rooms. I didn't see the body because we were all ushered back to our beds by Carlo and the police. I went to work as usual the next morning but, when I got back that night, the house had been closed down.

I was homeless again.

Luckily, I still had Malu. She helped me find a small studio flat in Edifício Copan, the same building that housed the salon. And she helped me with the deposit, which was three months rent in advance. Edifício Copan was one of the tallest buildings in Brazil, with thirty-eight stories, and it had the largest floor area of any residential building in the world. It had over a thousand apartments, ranging from small studios to large, five-bedroom units, and over two thousand residents. It had its own post code and there were seventy business establishments on the ground floor, including the salon I worked in, a church and four restaurants.

There were affluent parts of Edifício Copan and also poor parts. My flat was in the poorest part. The parquet flooring was broken and loose and electrical wires were exposed everywhere. There was a small kitchen and a tiny toilet covered in green mould. I was on the second floor and people threw rubbish out the windows of the thirty-six floors above me, onto a concrete patio at the back of the building. This rubbish was never cleared away and the smell came up and in through the two big windows of my flat that faced out that way. There were many suicides, with people jumping out the windows or off the roof, which was a hundred and forty meters high.

Despite the state of the flat, almost all my wages went on the rent and paying Malu back the deposit and although I was probably safer than I was in the shared house, I was still terribly unhappy. I would cry for nothing and sometimes I couldn't even speak – I could not find my voice. I asked myself over and over, why did my mother give birth to me? Did she not have enough children? Why did she have to have *me*? I thought about suicide again – about going up to the roof and jumping off with the others, but I couldn't even do that. I wasn't even able to end my miserable life. Malu helped me as much as she could. She shared her tips with me if I didn't get many of my own, and Adelena brought me food. Between the two of them, I just about managed to survive.

We got paid in cash at the end of each month and it was normal for us to keep the money in our lockers at work until we were going home. Then, one of the hairdressers had all her wages stolen from her locker and the police were called. They searched the salon, but the missing money could not be found. All the staff – apart from Malu and Adelena – pointed their fingers at me. They accused me because manicurists didn't earn very much, yet I had my own flat and, to them, I was living above my means. They didn't know that Malu and Adelena were helping me to survive. Also, I had confided in a girl called Natália and told her about my past, with Zylu and Laura and the other Mormons. She told the police I'd been accused of stealing before. As well as that, a client had given me a pair of earrings that I could never have afforded to buy myself. I'd gone to my flat that day with my two hands in my tabard and they said the missing money would probably be found there. All the evidence pointed to me. I was the obvious suspect.

The police arrested me and took me to the *delegacia de polícia* for further questioning while they searched my flat. I tried to answer all their questions and they wrote it all down, saying they would have to hold me while they checked my story, just in case I ran away. It took them a week and I was kept in a cell the whole time. I began to doubt myself and to wonder if I *had* taken the money. When you're depressed, you can't tell the difference between what is true and what is false. I was losing my grip on reality and everything around me became distorted. I saw menace everywhere, in every sound and shadow, and I cowered in a corner on the first night I spent in jail.

To my great relief, the police were not as bad to me as I had expected. They didn't beat me up and they gave me food. There was a toilet in the cell and they let me shower once during the week. After a while, I found myself thinking the place was nice; that I could stay there forever. I felt at peace. There was nothing to worry about. All my troubles were far away, on the outside of the strong walls. They could not get in to bother me.

I didn't expect to be let out; I expected to be blamed for the robbery and sent to prison for a long time. Even if I did get out, I would have no job and everyone would believe I was a thief – *again*. Then, after a week, the cell door opened and they said I could go. I was surprised, and a bit disappointed in a way. I didn't want to leave – to go back out there where my depression was waiting for me. But they had caught the real thief – it was Natália, the girl who had accused me. Her boyfriend was a cocaine addict and he was arrested by the police. Amongst other things, he gave her up as part of a deal to get a lesser charge of using, rather than dealing in, drugs. I went back to work, but the other girls treated me like I was dirt. Natália was their friend and I was not, and they still believed *I* was the guilty one. They came to the conclusion that I had somehow done a deal with a corrupt police officer – maybe offered him sex or something and passed the blame to her. Nasty comments and innuendo circulated loudly.

'Be careful of your belongings, girls.'

'I can't see why anyone would want to have sex with her.'

'I heard she had a police friend in Maringá.'

After a week of this treatment, I could bear it no longer. I ran crying to my flat. Malu followed and tried to console me, but I told her I could not come back.

For days, I just sat and stared at the walls, hardly moving, even to eat. Inertia engulfed me and a listless shroud hung from my shoulders. Then, after a while, clients started coming to the flat to have their nails done – one at first, followed by another, and then another. Malu had told them where I lived. Soon, a man called

Romeo came to see me. He ran a beauty salon close by and was looking for another manicurist. I don't know who told him about me – maybe it was Malu, or one of the clients – I never found out. Romeo's salon was more up-market than Terezanet and one of my clients was a woman called Stephanie. I believe in fate – in kismet – that things happened in my life because they were meant to. Stephanie came in every week and we would talk and talk. We were spiritually very similar and we got on really well. I felt comfortable with her and she said I was wasting my life as a manicurist. She asked if I would like to work with her, instead.

'Where?'

'A travel agency.'

'I don't know anything about that.'

'It's in the office. You'll be fine.'

Manicurists were ten-a-penny and to work in an office was a dream come true for a girl like me. It was considered "respectable" in Brazil – a step up the ladder. It was very exciting.

'Oh, yes please!'

In truth, it wasn't as glamorous as I thought. My starting salary was below minimum wage, so I couldn't afford my studio flat any more. I had to find shared accommodation again. This time it was a flat on the eighth floor of a big house in a smart area of the city. It had a balcony facing out onto the main road and was close to the office where I was working – just a ten-minute walk away. There were two bedrooms in the flat – I slept in one of them with the landlady and two other girls called Alexandria and Regina. The landlady and Alexandria had the two single beds, while I slept on the floor on a mattress, with Regina sleeping on the sofa. The other bedroom was occupied by the father of Bete Mendes, who was a big-time Brazilian TV star.

Apart from the bedrooms, there was a nice bathroom and a kitchen that we weren't allowed to use, so we had to eat out all the time, which was expensive. The landlady was called Olga. She had money, but she used to shoplift from stores and boast about it. She was proud of being able to get away with it and she would come home and show us what she stole that day.

I worked in the office from 8:00am to 5:30pm, Monday to Friday. In the beginning, I struggled with my new duties, especially typing letters, as my spelling wasn't great. Because of the drop in wages, I had to get a second job working evenings and weekends as a waitress in a bar. My starting time was 10:00pm, but I didn't get to finish until the last drunk left, and that could be as late as 5:00am. Despite working all those hours, I never had any spare money for anything because the cost of living in São Paulo was so high. I had to be well-dressed in the office and all my money went on work clothes and rent. Some days, I wouldn't be able to afford to have anything at all to eat. Because of this, my depression was not getting any better and the opportunity to go back to school seemed like an unreachable dream.

The manager of the bar was called Fabio. He was gay and his boyfriend was an African called Fernando, who claimed to be a *Candomblé* priest. *Candomblé* people believed that every person had their own individual spirit, which controlled their destiny. The spirit represented a certain force in nature and was associated with either food, an animal, a day of the week or a type of person – anything really. A person's character and personality was strongly linked to that spirit. I told him about my depression and Fernando said it was because I was being controlled by a bad spirit called *Boiadeiro*, who was a cowboy, and he could make it better. He made a hole in the neck of a live chicken and sucked the blood out – it was like he was in a trance and he became *Boiadeiro*. As the cowboy entity, he told me he loved smoking and he wanted me to carry loose tobacco round in my bag. I should also soak lots of tobacco in a bucket of water and wash myself in the solution. I should do this for several months. If I did this he, *Boiadeiro*, would be happy and my depression would go away. I did it once and the overpowering smell of the tobacco slop nearly made me faint and I had to get it off my skin as fast as I could. I also had to throw my bag away because of the stench and it was a while before I could afford another one.

I decided it was better to be depressed.

There was a birthday party in the bar one Saturday night and the people didn't leave until 7:00am the following morning. I missed the last night bus home and I sat on the pavement to wait for the first Sunday-morning bus to arrive. Tiredness overtook me and I fell asleep and didn't wake until noon, to find my bag and all my money had been stolen. I had nothing left. They even took my shoes. I started to walk the long way home, crying as I went. An old man with grey hair came up to me.

'Why are you crying?'

'I've been robbed. I have nothing left.'

He put his arms around me and gave me a hug. It was an act of kindness that made all the pent-up emotion flow out of me. In that moment, he was my mother, my father, my sisters and brothers; everyone I had ever loved in my life. He was an oasis of benevolence in a desert of misery. We embraced for a long while, a seventeen-year-old girl who was lost and alone and in desperate need of a hug from an eighty-five-year-old stranger – who was not a stranger. It was an act of unbearable kindness and not an obscene gesture as it might have seemed to an observer. He spoke again after a while and his voice was deep and comforting. It reminded me of the old *Curandeiro*, who lived deep in the forest.

'Are you hungry?'

'Yes.'

'I have a flat in Edifício Copan. Do you know it?'

'I used to work and live there.'

'I'll order you a pizza.'

I went back with him and we ate together. As we talked, I told him my story and he listened without interrupting. It was a big old-fashioned flat with lots of antiques – clean and homely and comfortable. The day passed quickly and it soon became late. We slept together in the same bed that night. He could not have sex because he was too old, but if he'd wanted to, I would have let him. I felt so grateful to him and I felt so safe in his bed. I wanted to stay there. *I could be happy here*. I thought to myself. *Comfortable. Safe. With someone who cares for me, who will buy me pizza without expecting the world in return.*

The next morning, I felt like I was somewhere I belonged. Again, I considered how lovely it would be to live there.

'Will you marry me?'

My question almost knocked him backwards with surprise. I knew he was lonely himself and it seemed like a perfect arrangement for both of us.

'I would love to marry you, but it would not be fair.'

'On you?'

'No. On you, Rozana.'

He said I was too young to be married to an old man like him, but I could stay as long as I wanted. He would take me to the seaside in summertime, where we could walk together in the waves and hold hands. He gave me a key so I could come and go as I wanted and a pair of shoes that belonged to his wife, who had been dead for forty years.

When I went back to the office I was so full of excitement and elation that I told Stephanie what had happened. She was horrified.

'Are you crazy, Rozana?'

'No, I . . . '

'He's a dirty old man. A paedophile!'

'No, he's not!'

She told me he would ruin my life and she was not going to let that happen.

'You say he lives in Edifício Copan. I'll report him to the police!'

'No! Please don't!'

'Then you must stay away from him.'

I didn't want to get him into trouble for nothing more than being kind and considerate.

Later that Monday, I put the key through his letterbox and never went back. I knew he would be deeply hurt. He would think it was fine while he was helping me, but the moment I didn't need him–

And I didn't even know his name.

Fabio paid me nightly for my work in the bar and I was able to struggle through until my next payday at the office. After my bad experience at the bus stop, I thought it would be safer to leave my money in the flat. I bought a lock for my wardrobe and went to work in the bar that night. When I came home in the early hours of the morning, my wardrobe had been broken into and all my money was gone, as well as my clothes. There was nothing left. I knew it wasn't Alexandria or Regina – so I believed it had to be Olga, the landlady who boasted and bragged about what she stole. I confronted her and she became very angry. She was much bigger than me and she punched me in the face and threw me out onto the street. She screamed at me, saying if I came near her door again she would call her sons and they would come and kill me.

Going to the police with no proof would mean it was her word against mine – and I already had a record. Even though I was never found guilty of anything, once you've been arrested in Brazil, it goes on a file that you have been accused of something and that information is available to investigating officers. Maybe Olga already knew this somehow. Maybe she knew one of the girls at Terezanet and saw me as an easy target. Maybe it was some kind of revenge for Natália – I never knew.

So I wandered away with nothing more than what I stood in – into the centre of the city, and it did what it threatened to do when I first arrived – dragged me down into its sordidness.

I felt sure I would never be seen again – until Hiago woke me and I went with him to Cracolândia.

CHAPTER TWELVE
STREET GIRL

Living in Cracolândia was like living in a war zone – with no rules. There was constant internal conflict between rival drug dealers and conflict between the people and the police, as well as external conflict between the homeless and so-called respectable society. The only real respect was between gang members.

My little group was called *"os sobreviventes,"* which meant "survivors" – and that's what we did. We survived. The gang was my only security in a place like Cracolândia. It was my family, my world, my sphere of existence. Without the gang, I would have died on the streets. I know I had survived on my own until then, but it was so different to Imbituva, Ponta Grossa or even Maringá.

In São Paulo, I did not have a prayer on my own. It was an unforgiving city, where everybody was trying to get by and no one had time to pick up those who fell over. Once you went down, you were trampled in other people's rush to get to the next rung of the ladder. If you slipped off the ladder, it was almost impossible to climb back up again. All you could hope for was to survive, but survival within the gang was survival based on fear. We were constantly afraid of the police, the drug dealers, the fire-bombers, and even afraid that we would wake up in the morning and the few possessions we had would be gone – stolen.

The kids used code words to communicate – police were *"cães,"* dogs – drug dealers were *"dragões,"* dragons – joy-riders were *"abutres,"* vultures – people they robbed were *"cabras,"* goats. They had their own language and they used it to evade police, to warn each other, to attack people passing by, and to communicate their friendship and loyalty to each other.

The nights were dark and dangerous, more dangerous than anywhere else I had been. The air was filled with screams, gunshots, revving car engines, police sirens and *pagode* and *forró* music from drunken street parties. It resonated with the bravado-speak of the boys and the strained, nervous laughter of the girls. The stink of various crack compounds pervaded the very air and overcame the odours of stale urine and faeces and decay. The days were different – they were filled with apprehension. The gang rose every morning and set out to find a "kill," much as a pack of wild animals would.

Luiz was our leader because he was the oldest, just a year older than me, and he motivated the rest, if the desire for crack was not enough motivation in itself. He howled in the morning, like an alpha wolf would howl, calling his pack to be ready for the hunt. Then we would trawl the destitute streets, looking for a lame duck, someone who had lost their way, a drunk, a degenerate – and if we could not find a prey who was weak enough, we would go into the city centre to pick pockets or pilfer from shops and street stalls.

It was a tenuous existence – one mistake and you were done for. The juvenile prisons were full to overflowing and life inside was brutal and hierarchical – that is if you managed to survive the police cells to get there. When I was detained before, I was not homeless – I had a job and a flat and an identity. That's why the police treated me with a degree of humanity. But they had no such tolerance for street kids, especially the ones from Cracolândia. To them we were rats, vermin – we polluted the city and needed to be exterminated. Street kids were raped and brutalised in police cells and nobody cared – not a single judge, lawyer, priest or politician. I sometimes thought of going back to the travel office, or to see Malu in the salon, but the longer I stayed, the more difficult it became to leave.

I didn't want to rob people and I avoided it as best I could. I stayed on the fringes of the gang, being used as a decoy, delivering drugs to people outside Cracolândia from the drug dealers inside, sometimes running guns from one source to another. I never knew who the supplier was or who the recipient was – and I never asked. It would have been more than my life was worth.

The membership of *os sobreviventes* changed regularly, some kids got killed or disappeared and other kids would take their places. They came with very little, but they shared what they begged or stole – even their drugs. They used crack cocaine to warm themselves up and make themselves feel better; to make life bearable. It was their panacea for every ailment – wounds, infections, hunger, fear and despair. To them, it cured everything – for a short while, at least. In actual fact, it cured nothing and caused everything.

The months rolled past and it was almost a year since Hiago took me off the wet city pavement and led me to Cracolândia. I was eighteen now and one of the oldest members of the gang. It was unlikely that I would be able to survive for much longer, but life had stagnated for me and I didn't care. I had achieved nothing since I set out from Lageado all that time ago. Every time I thought things were getting better, they just got worse again, so what was the point in even trying? At least in Cracolândia, there were no hopes, no dreams – and no disappointments. There was no way out of this place, and that suited me just fine. I had sunk down to the level where I belonged.

Ironically, the street kids called me "*princesa*" because I had looked so much cleaner and healthier than them when I first arrived – and the name stuck. As well as that, my depression went away, probably because I had far worse things to worry about than the size of my breasts or the fact that I had no money. I'm not saying my clinical depression wasn't genuine – it was – but in Cracolândia, clinical depression would be a minor condition compared to drug addiction, disease, starvation, murder, mutilation and the threat of being burned alive.

After that first year of existing in a living graveyard, I resigned myself more and more to the life of a street girl. My daily motivation was to avoid being killed, avoid taking drugs without being noticed, and to avoid being picked up by the police. Those were all negative and short-term objectives, but I had lost my motivation to make something of myself and my dream of making my mother proud had evaporated in the oppressive climate of hopelessness that constantly surrounded me. That's not to say I never laughed. I did – *we* did – in the way only young people can, excited about small things that would seem insignificant to others. Talking about the night ahead, or the previous night. Living lightly, with no possessions.

There were times when life seemed so ridiculous, when I traversed São Paulo with the gang and watched the tide of humanity ebbing and flowing across the city. All going somewhere that seemed so important to them, pushing and crushing to get there. While we watched from our futureless vantage point and laughed at them in a nervous, wishful-thinking way. And I felt a small sadness inside – an uneasy restlessness, like the world was closing in on me and it would never open up again.

Then a miracle happened.

A half-miracle.

I was begging in the Avenida São Luiz, near the travel agent office, with Dilma. It was late in the afternoon and people were on their way home from work. If they gave us money, it was thrown quickly at us as they hurried past, in case they might catch something from us – the desolate disease we suffered from. One person did not hurry past, but just stood there, casting a threatening shadow over our already invisible faces. I looked up and saw it was a woman. She was about twenty or so and looked vaguely familiar.

'Rozana?'

I could not put a name to the face, even though I knew her from somewhere. She bent closer with a hand over her mouth. I didn't know if this was in surprise, or in an effort to avoid contagion.

'Is that you, Rozana?'

I didn't answer. It could have been a trap. Dilma was on her feet and ready to run.

'It's me. Stephanie.'

Stephanie. That name was familiar – from another time. Another world. She caught my arm.

'Don't go.'

Dilma was already gone and I wanted to run after her, but Stephanie held on tight to my arm.

'I have some money for you.'

That aroused my interest and I stopped trying to break free. She took me to a roadside stall and bought me something to eat. I had holiday pay and some salary bonus coming from the travel agency office.

'Nobody could find you, Rozana, so I kept the money for you.'

'How much?'

'Five hundred reais.'

It was a great fortune to me in my present circumstances. Everything that was robbed or begged on the streets went to buy crack for the gang. There was never any money for anything else. We stole what we ate and lived mostly in the clothes we stood up in. This money was mine.

It was a lifeline.

Stephanie took me back to her flat in *Jardins*, a posh area of the city, where she lived with her two sisters, and gave me the money she'd been holding for me. She let me take a shower and she gave me some spare clothes, but the closeness we had before was gone. We were like strangers and I got the feeling she was a little afraid of me. I couldn't stay there because she didn't have room and the money I had was not enough to rent a place of my own. She kissed me and wished me well, but I could tell she was glad when I left – maybe she thought I might kill her in the night and take everything she had.

I left Stephanie's flat and wandered the streets on my own, my dirty Cracolândia clothes in a bag. I was facing a dilemma – should I try to get myself out of Cracolândia and resume the normal life that had now intruded so rudely on my aimless drifting? The life that, so far, had been a big disappointment and had made me clinically depressed and suicidal. Or should I go back to the gang, with whom I'd found a kind of contentment – a resignation to a short life that couldn't be changed and would come to a violent end very soon. I thought about it for a long time. I stopped to have a coffee in a small cafeteria and found a newspaper someone had left on the table. I automatically turned to the job pages.

Information technology was booming in Brazil at that time and a lot of companies were looking for telesales people to sell their products. I went to a local library and typed up a letter of application, using the business acumen I'd gathered from Rachel, and my poetic creativity. Then I changed back into my Cracolândia clothes and dirtied my face and messed up my hair. But I needed some place to hide my money and the clothes Stephanie gave me before I went back, otherwise I wouldn't have them in the morning. There was a building located between the city centre and Cracolândia where I knew the security guard. He was a go-between and I sometimes delivered drugs to him from the dealers for clients he had in his building. I had the money and clothes in a bag and I asked him if he could keep it somewhere for me.

'What's in it?'

'Just some clothes. They won't last long on the street.'

I opened the bag and showed him the clothes, but didn't say anything about the money. He took me down to a cellar underneath the building and told me I could hide the bag there.

'Could I use this address for a letter?'

'The cellar?'

'Yes, the cellar of this building.'

'Hmmm . . . what will you give me if I let you?'

'I can get you drugs.'

'Ok.'

I hid the bag where even the security guard wouldn't find it. Then I went back to Cracolândia.

The gang wanted to know who the strange woman was and how she knew my name. I told them she was a plain-clothes policewoman who had arrested me before I joined them. They were suspicious at first, but believed me when I described the conditions in a police cell. It even improved my street credibility. From then on, if I did stuff for the dealers and was rewarded with drugs, instead of distributing them to the gang members, I gave them to the security guard. This also improved my standing in Cracolândia, as now people believed I was taking the drugs myself and was truly one of them.

After a week or so, a letter came for me to the cellar address. It was a reply to my job application. I was invited to an open day with an IT company called RPS Informatica. I retrieved my clothes and money from the cellar and went to a public toilet to clean myself up. I looked respectable again, no longer like a dirty-faced urchin, but was I respectable enough to get the job?

There were hundreds of people at the open day and all the vacancies were gone by the time I got interviewed. My face fell.

End of miracle.

Then the lady who interviewed me asked me to wait outside for a moment. I could hear her on the telephone.

'We have a candidate we like, but no vacancies left. We don't really want to let her go.'

She waited while the person on the other end of the line answered. Then she spoke again.

'Yes, a very impressive application.'

Another silence while she waited.

'Good, that's excellent!'

Then she came and told me another branch of the company had a job for me.

I went back to the security guard and asked him if I could sleep in the cellar with my clothes for a few weeks.

'Why would you want to do that?'

'I have to keep out of someone's way at night. You know how it is.'

'You'll still bring me drugs?'

'When I can.'

'Ok, but you can't come until after midnight, and you must be gone by five in the morning.'

He didn't want any of the residents to know a street girl was sleeping in their building, even in the cellar. I agreed with his terms. The cellar floor was covered with thick black dust and it was full of rubbish and cobwebs. The security guard found me some cardboard to lie on and a sheet of plastic to cover me. A rat bit my toe on the first night sleeping there and I woke to find the rodents crawling all over me. I screamed and they ran back into their holes. It was nasty down there to say the least, but it was safer than being on the streets – rats or no rats.

The telesales company had a shower in the building so I got there early to clean myself up and get changed. After work I still had a lot of time to kill, so I changed back into my ragged clothes and rubbed dirt onto my face and messed up my hair before going back to Cracolândia. I continued to get peripherally involved in petty robbery and mugging every evening, along with distributing drugs, for which I would be paid with crack to give to the security guard. At midnight, I would disappear like Cinderella until the following evening. Every time I went back, one of the gang members would be gone – no one knew where – and a new kid would have joined. Very few of the original members of os sobreviventes remained, just myself, Hiago and Dilma. One-by-one, the others had been stabbed or shot or disappeared.

The IT company gave me a bus pass and daily luncheon vouchers, which I traded for cash to bring back to Cracolândia. This meant that when the others asked where "princess" had been all day, they believed me when I told them I went to a place I knew to rob rich people.

'We want to come with you.'

I told them I had a violent boyfriend and he would kill them if they came. To them, this was normal, so they didn't question it. Just in case, I sometimes used eye liner to blacken my eyes and I cut my arms with needles to make them bleed. I would push the needle right into my arm, then prise it up to break the skin. I even scratched the name "Robi" into my shoulder and told them it was the name of my boyfriend. I had to be very careful no one suspected I was leading a double life. They could have thought I was undercover police or an informer, and they would have killed me.

And so, for a while, I led a double life – selling terminals, printers, servers and processors during the day and robbing, begging and delivering drugs at night – until the witching hour, when I went back to sleep with the rats.

I thought I would be able to leave this double life when I got my first month's wages, but that wasn't the case. The telesales boss was a complete idiot and didn't have a clue how to manage a sales department. We never had the items people wanted to buy and he wouldn't listen to anyone's advice. As a big part of my wages was commission, it took me three months of going back onto the streets in the evenings and sleeping in the cellar at night before I finally made it out of Cracolândia.

CHAPTER THIRTEEN
DEPRESSION

I probably learned more during my time in Cracolândia than I would have in ten years at university – more about human nature, that is. The inexplicable contrast between the dark corners of society and the generosity of people with nothing to give, but who still open their hearts and offer their trust and friendship. I saw decadence and decency walking hand-in-hand. Goodness and badness standing together on the same street corner. Corruption and kindness in one pair of eyes. And I came to the conclusion that nobody was entirely bad, that everyone had a spark of humanity somewhere inside. It just needed to be nurtured for it to blossom and bloom into real virtue.

While I was with the gang in Cracolândia, the awful depression I had felt throughout most of my life left me. Maybe it was because I had worse things to worry about – or maybe my suicidal tendencies weren't real, just something that manifested itself when life seemed pointless. Ironically, life did not seem pointless in Cracolândia. On the contrary, it had an extra poignancy to it. It was more keenly felt, more sharply observed, and when I was out of there, I decided I had no right to be depressed. I would fight against it if it decided to come back.

When I had enough money, I looked in the newspaper and found shared accommodation again. It was a studio flat and quite small, but cheap enough for me to afford. There were three girls there already and they were looking for another to occupy the fourth bunk in the bedroom. Marcia and Eliane were both students in their early twenties and Mara was a part-time nurse. Apart from the overcrowded bedroom, there was a bathroom with a shower and a toilet, which we took turns in cleaning. But the kitchen was filled with thousands of cockroaches that we just couldn't get rid of, no matter what kind of insecticide we used. They kept coming back and smelled very strong when they swarmed and flew about everywhere. Marcia and Eliane didn't work, their parents paid the rent for them and sent them spending money every month. Mara was a drug addict who was going out with two different men. They both gave her money for sex and she hoped one of them would marry her some day.

After I had been there for a while, Mara told us she owed money to a drug dealer who said he would come round to the flat and kill us all if she didn't pay him. We didn't know if this was true or not, but we couldn't take the chance. So, between us, we found the money for her. Shortly after, she left and was replaced by Buana, who was about twenty-five and smoked cannabis all day. It was a challenge for me, living with these middle-class girls who didn't have to work and who wore the latest fashions and went out clubbing with their handsome boyfriends. They were living the life I dreamed of, while I was struggling to exist on the small commission I was earning in the telesales office. I felt the old symptoms of depression coming back, so to counteract them, I joined the *Cardecista* Catholics and went back into Cracolândia as a volunteer. I looked for Hiago and Dilma, but they weren't there – neither was anyone else I knew from my time as a street girl. I asked about them but nobody knew anything – nobody heard anything – nobody saw anything. That's just the way it was.

I became disillusioned with the charity work and felt there was no point to what I was doing there, handing out a bit of food once a week. What was needed was proper housing and jobs so they could help themselves. The fundamental need for education, common humanity and love meant that charity wasn't the answer, nor were handouts. I realised I wasn't really helping these people, just trying to help myself keep one step ahead of the spectre that was stalking me.

My recurring depression was always difficult for me to define or to quantify. A lot of people in Brazil thought it was just a way of being soft and weak, so I should snap out of it and pull myself together. Everybody feels a bit down now and then – a bit sad and fed up, but clinical depression is different, especially at its most severe. It doesn't just come for a little while and then leave, it stays for months on end.

My depression always made me feel hopeless and I would lose interest in everything, including myself. I was constantly tired and waves of suicidal thoughts would wash over me. Life would no longer be worth living and I would be plagued with feelings of guilt and low self-esteem. I'd had this illness before and I did not want it back. I thought I was free of it in Cracolândia, but I wasn't. It was still there, lurking in the shadows of my mind – waiting for me to emerge into what some people called normality.

After about six months I finally succumbed to the depression again. It wrapped itself around me like a blanket and kept me warm. It became my friend and comforted me in a friendless world. It kept me company in my loneliness. I embraced it like an obsession and grew to depend on it. With the depression came the low energy levels and lethargy. Most days I wished I hadn't woken up. Even things like taking a bath and talking became difficult.

I crawled from one day to the next. I sat in dark bars in the evenings with one drink in front of me, rather than go back to the flat and face the people I lived with, but had nothing in common with. I wanted to get back to my studies and maybe take evening classes or something, but I didn't have the energy to do it. The dark shawl of depression had closed itself round me once again and there was no way out of it.

One evening, I met a man named Marco in the bar. He was twenty-two and beautiful and I fell in love with him. It wasn't real love, of course, just some kind of emotional peg to hang my unhappiness on. He was a bit drunk and he kissed me and gave me his phone number, but when I called him the next day, he didn't remember me. That made me feel even worse than before.

I started eating pastries that I got from the stores in the evenings – stuff they didn't sell and were going to throw away. In just a couple of months, I put on fifty pounds and started self-harming. I cut myself with a knife to make the physical pain worse than the emotional pain. Once I drank a lot of alcohol, which I wasn't used to, and got really ill. The girls in the flat called the para-medics, who put a glucose drip into me. I was too drunk to realise what it was and when I twisted myself to be sick, the needle went right into my arm and I had to remain in hospital for a day, until they got it out and the swelling went down.

I would find myself standing on the *Viadulto 9 de Julho*, a bridge in São Paulo, trying to muster up the courage to jump off – but I didn't even have enough spirit to do that. It was like I was trapped inside my own body – a body with big ugly breasts that would not do what I wanted it to do. I longed to get out of it – to escape from it, but I didn't know how. I hungered for more education. I would walk past the university and imagine myself going there. I cried for a good job that paid more than the minimum wage. I prayed for a nice house and a nice family. All those things seemed so far away, so unachievable, that I could not see the point in trying to reach for them.

My levels of energy were so low at this time that even feeling sorry for myself was hard work. I was listening to the *want* static – desiring things I thought I deserved and getting frustrated and despondent when I could not have them.

I was in my third year of living in São Paulo and I was about to turn twenty. I had a job that barely allowed me to survive, a clinical depression that made me suicidal, a poor education by average standards, and I was fifty pounds overweight. The dreams

I had when I wrote to my mother, what seemed such a long time ago, felt further away than ever. Yet deep down inside, a voice was constantly telling me that something good would happen. It would all come right if I had the patience to wait.

That was the problem. I didn't want to wait. I wanted it to happen right away.

During a rare moment of hope I found *Madre Vicunha*, a very exclusive school for rich girls during the day that ran cheap classes for poor girls like me in the evenings. I started to attend those classes to get the level of education equivalent to high school GCSEs. However, due to lack of concentration caused by anxiety and depression, I failed my exams in the first year. The failure seemed to awaken some latent determination and strength and although I still felt suicidal, I needed to prove what I could do. I told myself I either wanted this or I didn't! I had to stop blaming the world for everything and get on with it. No one else was going to do it for me.

The melancholy did not go away – clinical depression doesn't do that. But I found a way round it by deciding it was my enemy, not my friend, and I had to fight it to get what I wanted. This new determination gave me the motivation to carry on, to give more than I thought I had in me to my studies.

The hard work paid off. I passed my exams the second time round and that opened up the way to further education. I just had to find a better job. I had worked in sales for a while and despite of my poor qualifications, I composed a brilliant CV, exaggerating the truth as much as possible. I had it typed up at the library and applied for an executive sales job with a flooring company called *Maximiliano Gaidzinsk S/A*, located in a new commercial area of *Jardins*. To my surprise, I was given an interview, so I bought myself a cheap suit and went along.

I arrived early to make a good impression, but there were already over a hundred people waiting to be interviewed. A man called Renato came out – he was something of a celebrity in Brazil – a tall, blue-eyed model and footballer. He was holding a microphone and he asked for our attention. He talked about the company for a while and said there were ten vacancies, and preference would be given to those candidates with university degrees. On my CV, I had said I was studying for exams to enter university, but that was a lie. I spoke to some of those around me – they all had either finished their degree courses or were still at university. Some were even post graduates. My chances seemed very slim.

I was one of the first to be seen. There were four people in the interview room, three males and one female, all dressed in expensive suits and looking really important. The woman and one of the men asked questions, one of the others took notes and the fourth just sat there observing. They asked me about my work experience, my personal life, my aspirations and what I liked to do in my spare time. I tried to stay upbeat and didn't mention that, until recently, I'd been living with crack addicts and I sometimes felt like jumping off the *Viaduto 9 de Julho*.

The interview lasted about half an hour and, at the end, the man who had been observing asked me why he should give me a job. I didn't really know what to say, but I had to say something. I smiled.

'If you give me the job, you won't need to see anyone else and you can have the afternoon off.'

They all laughed and looked at each other, as if they didn't know what to make of me. The quiet man spoke again.

'Before we finish, if I asked you to compare yourself to an animal, which animal would it be?'

'A cow.'

They were silent for a moment, then they all laughed again. Louder this time. I felt stupid for saying that – but I loved cows.

When the laughter died down, they asked me to wait outside. I wanted to go home because I believed I had made a fool of myself and had no chance of being picked. I waited most of the day, with other people joining me from time to time. At the end of the interviewing, there were about forty of us waiting. One of the men came out and said they would like to see us all again tomorrow. I was amazed. I must have made a good impression after all!

The next day, I was the first to arrive. One of the men who carried out the interviews the previous day saw me. He looked at the clock on the wall.

'Somebody's early.'

The second round of interviews began when all the others had arrived. I was the first to be called into the room.

'Ah, the young lady who is like a cow.'

They smiled at each other, then at me. The quiet man spoke first.

'Could you explain that?'

'Well cows have a friendly nature, don't they?'

'I suppose so.'

'They are strong and clever.'

'Are they?'

'Oh yes. And they're extremely useful, and a great source of food. Nothing from a cow goes to waste.'

The quiet man thought to himself for a moment.

'I've never seen cows in quite that way before, but I suppose you're right.'

The four of them whispered amongst themselves for a short while, then the female spoke.

'You realise you're competing with very strong candidates, Rozana.'

'Yes, I realise that.'

'So, why should we pick you?'

I looked straight at the quiet man, because I knew he was the decision maker.

'Because I'm like the cow. I have just the right temperament to deal with the public. I'm strong and clever enough to adapt to most situations and working environments. I will be a great source of inspiration to those around me and I will use all my resources for the benefit of the company. Nothing will be wasted.'

'The other candidates might do the same.'

'Did any of them compare themselves to a cow?'

'Well . . . no.'

The quiet man smiled at me and rose to his feet. He asked me to wait outside again.

I prepared myself to wait all day but, after ten minutes, I was called back into the room. The female spoke.

'If we give you a job, Rozana, would you be available to go away on a week's training course?'

'Yes. Yes, I would!'

'Very well. Welcome to the team.'

For the first time since I arrived in São Paulo, I began to believe I could actually achieve something – make something of myself.

I was so excited.

The week-long course was to take place in a city called Joinville in the southern Brazilian state of Santa Catarina. Despite having few clothes to pack, my confidence was high and I waited for Monday morning in great anticipation. All ten chosen candidates assembled outside the company head office in *Jardins* at 6:30am. Our coach was already there. My new colleagues looked very smart and professional and my inferiority complex began to rear its ugly head as I approached them. I felt uncomfortable and lowly, like I didn't belong there. They were mingling and getting to know each other – asking about each other's lives, where they lived, their families, their education, where they had travelled. I didn't want to talk to them because I knew I would have to lie to compete with them. Some were saying how hard the interviews had been and how their qualifications had helped them get hired. I tried desperately to find a niche in the conversation, but what could I say – I got chosen because I compared myself with a cow? They would have laughed till they cried.

The coach departed at 7:30am and the trip took nine hours

altogether. On the way, we stopped for lunch at a really nice restaurant near Curitiba, where Rudolfo lived. I wondered if I might see him and I could say, "I'm the girl you thought was Charlene," but he wasn't there.

A table had been booked for us and each place had a name on a white cardboard card. Seeing my name there with the others made me feel very important and I began to feel confident again – until the waiter brought the menu. I had never even heard of most of the dishes on there – appetizers like *isca de peixe* and *coracao de galinha* and main courses like *vaca atolada* and *peito de franco grelhado*. I waited for the others to order first, pretending to be seriously considering my choices, and ended up with *bifé cavalo*, which was steak with fried egg, served with potatoes and a side salad and a glass of coke to wash it down. When the food was served, I waited again, to see which knives and forks the others used, then I copied them.

We arrived at our hotel in Joinville at 6:30pm. It was a four-star hotel and more beautiful than anything I had ever seen. We were told to go to our rooms and have a shower, then meet up in the hotel restaurant at 7:30pm for dinner. The rooms were twinned, with two single beds in each and a discussion developed to decide who was going to share with who. I just kept quiet, too scared of being rejected. I ended up with Lydia, a young architect who had just left university. She was Japanese-Brazilian, cultured and very delicate looking – more Japanese than Brazilian. We got along very well and became friends and sat together at dinner.

Lydia showed me how to order and what cutlery to use and I soon believed I was as sophisticated as the rest of them – even if I wasn't.

Most of the week was spent in one of the hotel's conference rooms, where we learned a lot of sales related techniques – like body language and how to make customers trust you and make people buy from you. On one occasion, we went for an outing to the company's factory in Joinville to familiarise ourselves with their flooring products. In the evenings, we had a variety of literature to study and the time went quickly for me. Being part of it and being treated like someone special was a dream. I had to pinch myself, for it didn't seem real.

The training course finished on Friday lunchtime and we were given the afternoon off to explore the city. Joinville was the largest city in Santa Catarina State. Many of the people were German and it had one of the highest standards of living in South America. It was filled with churches and museums and it had a ballet company, a botanical gardens and a zoo. I marvelled at it all and allowed it to seep into my soul, until it was time to get back to the hotel and set off for São Paulo.

The journey back was less formal and more fun than the trip down there. We all knew each other by then so we chatted and sang and, much to my surprise, I seemed to be quite popular. It was early Saturday morning when we arrived back, and we went our separate ways to prepare ourselves for our new lives, which would begin on Monday morning.

The first week was very challenging. There were so many tiling and flooring products and I had to get to know them all if I was going to be as good as my word to the interviewers. All the newcomers stuck together for the first few days and I noticed they were all just as lost as me.

There was a meeting on the Monday of the second week and we were told that each sales executive would be given several exclusive clients to look after. We would be based at the premises of those clients and we would have set sales targets to reach. I was given two clients – one of them was *Telhanorte* and the other one was *Madeirence do Brazil*, two companies that sold a wide variety of home improvement products. I was the *Maximiliano Gaidzinsk S/A* representative in their chains of stores and this is where the job became really complicated. Not only did I have to be familiar with my own company's products, but also with *Madeirence do Brazil's* and *Telhanorte's* even wider range of goods and services.

I had my own team of sales promoters, with separate stands for kitchens, living rooms, toilets and balconies – everywhere flooring or tiles could be laid. Our target rate was 250,000 square meters of flooring and tiling per week and I supervised it all. I had a very good basic salary, well above minimum wage, along with an excellent commission percentage and bonus on sales.

I didn't reach my targets in the first month, even though I got paid more than I ever believed possible. The second month was much better, because there was a boom in new houses and we sold massive amounts of material to the rich people who were building them. I started to believe I was born to be a sales executive. I loved it. The company invested very heavily in training and we would have a full day's tutoring every three months, along with a week away at a conference hotel at least once a year. I continued my evening classes with *Madre Vicunha* during this time, Monday to Friday, taking mathematics, science and general studies, along with the compulsory catholic religion.

During my first year with the company, I found out where Marco was living and I rented a studio apartment in the same building. It was a nice place in a fashionable area, but very expensive. I bought some trendy clothes and sent my mother money to help her build a better house, along with a letter.

> *Dear Mãe,*
> *I have been gone a long time, I know. But I am*
> *beginning to make something of myself, as I*
> *promised you. You are hearing from me because*
> *I have started to do what I needed to do. I hope*
> *you have not worried about me. I am keeping my*
> *promise to make you proud. I am getting there.*
> *Your loving daughter,*

Rozana.

To my surprise, I received a reply. I knew my mother couldn't write, but she had asked someone to send me a letter on her behalf. It said simply –

Dear Rozana,
I am already proud of you.
Never forget that.
Mãe

I read the short note with tears rolling down my cheeks.

CHAPTER FOURTEEN
STARVATION

Becoming Marco's neighbour was something I had planned on doing from the moment I met him in that bar, when he kissed me and gave me his phone number – even though he did not remember me the next day. I believed if he had the opportunity to get to know me, he would fall in love with me and we would live happily ever after. It was a complete illusion, of course, a hopeless hope. Had it actually come true, I would have found out that living ever after with him had nothing to do with love. It might have something to do with movement and smell and taste and touch and violence and sound and sense and light and dark and addiction and compulsion and hope and despair.

People loved their mothers, their children, their dog. That thing between a man and a woman had nothing to do with love. Did it?

When we met in the lift for the first time, he didn't recognise me. I was disappointed and became over eager – began "accidentally" bumping into him on the stairs far too often, sending him a breakfast basket he never even thanked me for, giving him my apartment number, though he never visited. I decided I wasn't doing enough to attract his attention. I was still overweight, so I had to go on a diet. A normal diet, where I would lose three or four pounds a week, wasn't quick enough for me. I wanted to be slim right away!

I was due a few weeks' holiday from work and instead of going on a trip somewhere or doing something interesting, I decided to stay at home and starve myself.

On the first day I ate and drank nothing. Not even water. The next day, the lack of energy filled me with self doubt – I wouldn't be able to do this. What was the point? I was ugly. I would only disappoint myself again. The demons were still there. I was still alone, and I always would be.

Nothing was real except the impenetrable depression. But the determination that had spurred me on to pass my exams stirred inside me and kept me going.

I ate and drank nothing on the second day, or the third, or the fourth. By the end of that week I had lost twenty pounds. I felt ill and could hardly get off the bed, but I had no yearning for food.

During the second week, I had a few sips of water, but not much, because I believed it would bring my appetite back. By the end of that week I'd lost the fifty pounds it took me months of eating pastries to put on, but I was unable to walk without holding onto the walls. My hands were shaking and it felt like every organ in my body was convulsing with cold. I was also beginning to hallucinate – seeing spectres in the night and demons during the day. It was becoming more and more difficult to determine what was real and what was surreal, and I was frightened.

I thought I was going to die, but I didn't want to. Before, when I was depressed, suicide was always sitting on my shoulder, whispering in my ear. I had either managed to resist it, failed in my attempts or simply didn't have the energy to jump. Suddenly, these impulses were strangely absent. Maybe it was just a matter of suicide seeming like a dramatic option, a grand gesture, an impressive exit. Until the time came to actually do it. Then it grew sordid and ugly and tragic, in the worst possible way.

I realised that my previous suicidal tendencies were a type of attention seeking. If I died in theatrical circumstances, people would talk about me and I would have their attention – if only for a while. But to die ignominiously in my apartment like this would not have the desired effect. No, I had to live. Suicide could come at a more convenient time.

With great difficulty, I managed to get to a public telephone and call a friend from work. When she saw me, she hardly recognised me. I told her what I had done. She immediately called for an ambulance and I was rushed to hospital. They took blood samples, which showed I was severely malnourished and had developed anaemia. They kept me in there for nearly a week and put me on a course of vitamins and a drip-feed, because I wouldn't eat the slurry they served me. I think I might have developed anorexia at that time. I saw food as an enemy; a threat. I knew I was ill and would die if I didn't eat, but I just couldn't. I had taught myself how to go without food and now it was difficult to learn how to eat again. The new, skinny Rozana was petrified of getting fat again.

I was feeling a bit better when they let me out of the hospital and I went to a shop and bought a lettuce, an apple and a low-fat yogurt drink. I stayed on that diet for days, but at work, it was a struggle to cope and it affected my evening classes. I lost another year. My work colleagues hardly recognised me, they thought I had cancer or Aids or some other terminal disease. It was hard for me to motivate my sales team because I had no energy and couldn't even motivate myself. I felt very weak all the time, as if I was going to pass out – and I did, in front of a client.

Everything went black and I fell over onto my face. An ambulance was called and, at the hospital, I was told if I didn't start eating properly, I would not see my next birthday. I weighed less than six stone.

I was a good salesperson and *Maximiliano Gaidzinsk S/A* did not want to lose me, but I was in danger of getting fired if I carried on the way I was going. It was the point of no return for me – it was eat or die! So I started to eat – slowly at first. Painfully. Emotionally. Psychologically.

As my physical health improved, my emotional state deteriorated. I became jealous of happy people – those about to get married, young couples holding hands, families buying stuff for their homes. I wanted all of that, a loving husband and children and a nice house to live in, but it still eluded me.

On the other hand, things at work were improving all the time. I developed a great relationship with my clients, my boss was professional and fair, and money was not a problem anymore. As well as that, my studies picked up and it wouldn't be long until I finished my high school exams.

So, why did I feel so despondent?

I tried to explain it to myself, to rationalise it – but it wasn't rational. There was no logic in the darkness. I stumbled about in it, trying to find a reason, a rationale. I was a clever girl and I should be able to cope with life, but I couldn't. I looked for excuses. I hadn't seen my family for seven years and I had been through a lot on my own. Maybe that was the problem. Maybe it was the weather – the wind – the birds in the trees. I didn't know until years later, when I was diagnosed.

Just before I turned twenty-four, my boss called me into a meeting and announced that the National Merchandising Director was due to retire and he wanted me to prepare to take the job. I was their best salesperson, I never complained, nothing was too difficult for me, and the clients liked me.

'And you must be due to finish university soon, Rozana?'

'My course was delayed.'

I lied.

In reality, I had just completed my pre-college exams and hadn't even entered university, which I told them I was ready to do when they employed me.

'No matter. I believe you are the perfect candidate and you will be a great asset to the company in your new role.'

They sent me on a six-month training course. The company had five factories in different parts of Brazil – one in Espirito Santo, one in Minas Gerais and three in Santa Catarina. I had to spend a month at each of them, as well as a month back at the office in São Paulo. It was like a new life. I was travelling everywhere by plane and being picked up by private chauffeur-driven cars. I stayed at the best hotels and went to parties with company managers and supervisors.

The role of National Merchandising Director entailed developing and training sales teams and travelling around the country to showrooms in different States. The company also sent me to study interior design at a Pan-American school in São Paulo. I started in my new job after the training period was over and it was very exciting to begin with.

I was so busy during the days that I forgot about my depression but, gradually, in the evenings, it crept back over me and I was another sad person with no real friends and no family. I had a lot more than many people in Brazil – I was on my way to reaching the material goals I'd always aspired to and I couldn't understand why I was still so dissatisfied with my life. Sometimes it seemed to me that I was happier when I was a young child in Lageado, with nits and worms and rashes, or when I was on the streets with the *crianças de rua* in Cracolândia.

I moved into a bigger flat in the *Jardins* area in 1997. It was very expensive and close to the company offices, with a proper kitchen and clean bathroom, a spacious living room and a bedroom that was big enough for two people. I bought all brand new furniture before I moved in, but I still felt lonely.

Luana was a work colleague who lived in a shared flat that had cockroaches, so I invited her to move in with me, just to see if she would be able to help get me out of my miserable mood. Unfortunately, Luana caused more problems than she cured. She took advantage of my emotional isolation and unhappiness and exerted an influence over me that was manipulative and domineering. Luana had a strong personality and she used people with subtle psychological bullying.

My personal confidence was low, despite my job and my prospects. I was vulnerable and just wasn't able to cope with her.

She gave up work and expected me to pay all the bills. I threatened to evict her, or to leave, but she always got round me, behaved for a while and told me she loved me, then she would revert to her old self after a few days.

She began throwing parties that I footed the bill for, but they were always her friends, not mine, and I felt left out. Except for a man called Ricardo Sirimarco, who was older than the rest – in his late forties. He was an artist who had some kind of secret job in the government, or so I imagined. We formed a tentative friendship that grew stronger and lasted down through the years, even to the present day.

Back then, he used to socialise a lot with Luana and her friends and he often asked me to accompany them when they went out, but Luana always objected.

'Oh no, Rozana wouldn't enjoy D Edge.'

'Well, she might.'

'She wouldn't. Would you, Rozana?'

'I don't know, I . . .'

'See. I told you!'

I was finding it increasingly difficult to cope, so I began to take Valium. Just a small dose at first, which made me feel infinitely better. It was a miracle cure for my moroseness, and it also gave me the confidence to decide I could not live with Luana and her parasitic lifestyle any more. So I left her in the flat and moved into a smaller place on my own. It was a comfortable one-bedroom flat in a nice area. Luana couldn't afford my flat when I moved out, but I had paid three months' deposit, so she stayed there until that term ran out.

Lucia was a rich girl I'd met when I was working in the salons. We became friends and I kept on doing her nails after I left. She wanted to have a breast reduction, but was scared of the operation. So she offered to pay for me to have the procedure first, if I told her what it was like afterwards. Now, I had always hated my large breasts, so I jumped at the offer. I booked four weeks' holiday from work. Lucia took me to a private clinic in São Paulo. She paid £4,000 and I had the breast reduction. I know it sounds perverse, with so many women wanting breast enlargement these days, but it was what I craved for. Finally, I would have the shape I always wanted. I would no longer be top-heavy and gauche. I would be elegant and svelte and people would pause to look at me when I passed – or so I imagined.

The operation went without complication, but I couldn't move my arms for four weeks afterwards and I couldn't get out of bed without my neighbour's help. Even when I went back to work, I was badly bruised and very sore for about six months. Lucia saw how much pain I was in and she decided not to go through with her own operation. Ironically, there was nothing wrong with my breasts, the abnormality was in my head. But the operation had the desired effect and my smaller breasts boosted my self-confidence. They made me feel like a different person.

I changed my wardrobe and hairstyle and bought myself a new car, even though I didn't know how to drive. When Luana found out I had the car, she began to invite me out with her, just so I could drive her places. I refused at first, but I wanted to see Ricardo and my friendship with him deepened. It was like with Marcelo – Ricardo was a kind and intelligent and sophisticated man and it was always a pleasure to be in his enlightened company, even if I had to put up with Luana as well.

The car was an Opel Corsa and it was a beautiful little machine. I was very proud of it. I had never driven before and when I went to collect it, a friend from evening class came with me. She got the car out of the showroom and onto the road, then I took over. I accelerated into the car in front, then drove it erratically home, hitting the wing mirrors of several parked vehicles along the way. After that, I just bought a driving licence from a corrupt instructor and I was ready to go.

I practised pedal control in the ground-floor garage of the block of flats where I lived and when I was confident enough, I decided to take it out onto the roads. It took me five hours to get the car out of the garage and I scratched both sides badly in doing so. I stalled the Corsa numerous times while I was out and I had many motorists hooting their horns and shaking their fists at me. When I parked it, I forgot to put the handbrake on and it started to roll down a hill. Luckily, a man chased after it for me and managed to jump inside to stop it. He gave me a lecture and told me to learn how to drive before I killed someone! I persevered with practise, continuing to crash into parked cars and stall the vehicle – for many weeks. I split the tyres almost every day from driving up onto kerbs but, gradually, I got better. At least, I wasn't a danger to the public anymore.

I decided I'd had enough of being moody and morose and I began to live life to the full, clubbing every weekend and going to the beach in a bikini, which I'd never done before. After a while of feeling free of my depression, I decided to give up taking the Valium. Then I met Marco again in a bar and he showed some interest in my new image. We went out a few times and had sex, but to my disappointment, he told me he didn't want a serious relationship.

This brought the old sadness and self-consciousness back. It began to stalk me like it had before, following me around, waiting for me to be alone so it could come and violate me. I did not want to go back on the tablets because the dose I was taking had been increasing and I was told they could become addictive. So I decided to go home for a holiday at Christmas to cheer myself up. I wrote a letter to my mother so she would know to expect me. I had written to her several times over the years and always sent money, but I had only ever received one reply – when she said she was already proud of me. So, I didn't know quite what to expect.

CHAPTER FIFTEEN
KIDNAPPED

It was Christmas of 1998 and nearly nine years since I had been back to Lageado. During the time I was away, I had grown from a girl approaching seventeen years of age, to a woman approaching twenty-six.

I had changed a lot. I'd travelled all over Brazil, earned money, been promoted in my job, become better educated and recently started driving my own car – badly.

I hoped my mother would be proud of what I had achieved and we could have a happy time together. I decided to drive home to show off my skills, down the *Rodovia Regis Bittencourt*, which was known as the "motorway of death." It was one of the most dangerous roads in South America, with many accidents involving big speeding lorries. Even though it was called a motorway, it only had two lanes and oncoming traffic could swerve all over the place in wet, water-spraying weather.

The journey home was a ten-hour nightmare of honking horns, screeching brakes, smoking tyres, loud swearing and shaking fists. My heart was beating so fast that I had to pull over onto the hard shoulder several times to calm down and stop myself from shaking.

Eventually, I made it.

I drove into Lageado at about 6:00pm. The village had changed – it was bigger than I remembered. There was electricity now and the new motorway, a few cars driving round and a bus service twice a day to Ponta Grossa and places in between.

My family was still poor, but they had a bigger and better house now, which they'd built themselves. It had a tiled floor and the walls were painted blue. There were two bedrooms, a living-room, a toilet and a balcony. They even had furniture – proper beds and a sofa and cupboards and a table with wooden benches. But there were no appliances – cooking was still done over an open fire and clothes still washed in the stream.

My mother was pleased to see me, but she looked very different from when I left, nine years earlier. Her hair was completely grey, her face was wrinkled and she was bent over. She walked with difficulty from the back problems she had from constantly working in the fields. My mother had never looked young, not that I could remember at least – her hair was always grey and she never had any teeth. But now she looked very old, and she could only have been in her late fifties, although she had no birth certificate and never knew her real age. Her back problems were chronic, with pain shooting down her leg – the legacy of a life spent supporting her family. A life of hardship that was taking its toll on her physical health.

My brothers and sisters treated me like a stranger. They were all at home, either working for the Germans or renting plots of land to farm for themselves. I wanted to show myself off – my clothes, my accent, my make-up, my hair and my car – but they weren't impressed. They found the way I spoke without swearing strange, and the fact that I could use a knife and fork made them think I'd become a snob.

'We used to pull the worms from your nose when you were little, Rozana. Have you forgotten that?'

To my horror, I discovered that my younger sister Nicole was now living with Paulo Oliviera, who tried to rape me when I was eleven, and she lived with him as his wife in Palmar. He and Karina got divorced and he came to live in Lageado. My sister Nicole had a baby for an older man in the village when she was thirteen and she would have been treated very badly if it had not been for Paulo. He looked after her and gave her respectability. When I met him again, he didn't seem to remember doing anything bad to me, so I said nothing about it – for Nicole's sake.

My father was sixty-two now and he was very ill. He was not able to walk at all and he couldn't eat properly because the food hurt his throat. Everyone thought it was just some kind of infection, but I knew it was more than that. I took him to the hospital in Curitiba, where they did some tests. A few days later he was diagnosed with terminal throat cancer. I loved my father almost as much as I loved my mother. He was an easy-going man who danced with me and made me laugh when I was little. He told me stories and jokes and I called him "papi."

'Who is this papi, Rozana? I know no papi.'

'You are.'

'Am I?'

And he would laugh.

He wasn't laughing anymore.

He wasn't dancing or telling jokes, and I missed all the years I hadn't spent with him. I couldn't stand seeing him so fragile, knowing there was nothing I could do about it. The doctors decided to operate on him so he could eat better and his last few months would be easier to bear. Then Christmas was over and it was time for me to go back to work. I left my car there to help make life easier for my father, and I took the bus back to São Paulo.

My father got an infection after the operation and he died two weeks later.

I took the bus back to Lageado again. There was a wake, like with Ramon all those long years before. My father's coffin was placed on the table with a veil covering him inside it.

Worse than losing my father was seeing my mother's devastation. She never knew her parents because she was orphaned as a baby. She was brought up as a servant by another family, who treated her like a slave from the time she was very young. My father took her away from that when she was thirteen and they had been together ever since. He was the first real person she had ever known, the kindest person she had ever known, the most easy-going person she had ever known, and she loved him.

Now he was gone.

She would not leave his side and cried constantly until they came to take him to the church. I'd never seen my mother cry like that before and I wanted to hug her, but she wouldn't let me. She would not be consoled.

They put my father's coffin onto a lorry and many people climbed aboard. They went to the church first, I don't know why, there was no priest – my mother couldn't pay for one. She was just hanging onto the coffin – crying, crying, crying. There were blisters on her face from the tears. Then they took my father to the cemetery and buried him while the people around the grave prayed and my mother sobbed. She cried louder with every shovel-full of earth that thudded down onto the coffin lid. In the end, she had to be led away by my sisters.

I couldn't bear to witness my mother's grief, so I went back to São Paulo straight after the funeral. The first thing I did was go to a bar to have a drink, trying to forget the terrible pain in my mother's face.

I felt utterly alone.

I was never a heavy drinker, so I just had a beer and I drank it very slowly. Then I had another. Apart from grieving for my father and fretting for my mother, I was doubting myself as well. I had missed out on so much at home, and for what? I had a good job, a decent flat and a car, but not much else.

After a while, I noticed a man watching me from another table. He was about thirty, good-looking and wore glasses. An hour or so later, when he was sure I wasn't there to meet anybody, he came across. I wasn't drunk, but I had not eaten anything for quite some time and the alcohol was beginning to have a balming effect on my troubled mind.

'Hello.'

'Hello.'

'My name is Hugo. You look sad.'

'I am sad.'

'Why?'

He sat down without being invited and I told him my father had died. He was sympathetic. He said I was too young and pretty to be so sad and he could cheer me up.

'How?'

'With a *magica*.'

He went to the bar and brought back two cocktails. I tasted mine, it was delicious.

'What's in it?'

'A mixture of cachaça and choi tea, with orange and lemon.'

'It's lovely.'

'Just like you.'

By the time I had finished the cocktail, I was feeling a bit dizzy. I decided it was time to go, but I couldn't get to my feet. I was aware of what was going on around me, but found it incredibly difficult to move.

'Are you alright, Rozana?'

'I can't . . . seem . . . to . . . '

'You've probably had too much alcohol. I have a car outside. Let me take you home.'

He picked up my bag and started to lift me from my seat. The barman came across.

'Is everything alright?'

'She's had too much to drink.'

I could hear people talking around me, but I couldn't speak myself. Hugo carried me out of the bar and put me into the back of his car. Nobody tried to stop him.

Then everything went black.

I have no idea how long I was unconscious but, when I came to, I was on a bed in a room with no windows. My head was splitting and I felt groggy, but I managed to get to my feet. I could hear loud music coming from the next room. It was a song by a heavy metal band called *Sepultura*, which means a grave or tomb. I went towards it. The music was overpowering and coming from a CD player in a kitchen. There was a window, but it was boarded up. Hugo was in the room next to a wooden table, cutting something with a large knife. He must have sensed me, because he spoke without turning.

'Are you hungry?'

'Where am I?'

He turned and looked at me with a leer. When I met him in the bar, he was wearing glasses. Now he wasn't and his eyes were wide and protruding. He looked weird and wild and his voice was low, like a growl.

'You're home, Rozana.'

He was cutting a pizza with the knife and singing along to the dark music. I was very frightened now.

'I want to go home.'

He began to slide his hand along the edge of the knife, while smiling at me in a manic kind of way.

'I told you, you *are* home.'

I decided it was best to humour him. I had been suicidal and wanted to die many times in my life, but not now. It's strange, is it not – people think they want to die, but when death is staring them in the face, when it is so close they can feel its stinking breath on their neck, then it ceases to be quite so appealing.

I have to say, for the benefit of the readers of this book, the horrors that happened to me in that place will not be easy reading. My hand is trembling as I write and I feel ashamed and sick and violated all over again. So, if you do not have a strong stomach, you should skip to the next chapter.

As I said, I decided to humour Hugo until I could find a way out of wherever I was. I went to the table and ate a slice of pizza, even though it almost choked me. He smiled at me when I finished it, as if I had been a good girl.

'You should take a shower now.'

'I don't want to.'

His mood changed immediately. He grabbed me by the hair and dragged me to the shower. He turned it on and threw me under the stream, still holding the knife.

'Take off your clothes!'

I did and he took them away with him. When he came back, he was naked as well and he got under the shower with me.

He began to bite me – on my arms, my shoulders, my neck and my back – all over. I was terrified, but I didn't try to fight him because I got the feeling it would have excited him even more. He was a big man, much bigger than me, and I would have been no match for him.

'I want you to shit.'

'What?'

'Shit!'

'I can't . . .'

He grabbed my face and forced my mouth open and shoved some kind of tablet down my throat. Then my bowels opened and I could not stop myself from defecating. He forced me to bend over and he began to eat the faeces that came out of me. It was all over his face and he was making noises like an animal. I began to vomit. I spewed up until there was nothing left inside me and my stomach was hurting.

I ran from the shower. He didn't follow me. I ran round the house or apartment or whatever it was, trying to find a way out, but the heavy security door was locked and there was only one window in the kitchen area, which was boarded. I started to scream – somebody might hear me and come to my rescue. Nobody did and my screams echoed back, as if they were trying to make their own escape.

I tried to pull the boards off the window with my bare hands but they were screwed on securely and I couldn't budge them. There were narrow cracks between the boards and when I looked through, I could see it was dark outside. We were high up, about thirty feet, and the nearest lights were some distance away. I looked for the knife he was cutting the pizza with, but the next thing I knew, I was grabbed from behind and dragged into the bedroom.

For the rest of that night, I was repeatedly raped with a multitude of implements – sex toys and a glass bottle and other things were inserted into me. I was crying and bleeding and it was like a scene from hell. He inserted things into himself as well and made unnatural noises, the like of which I had never heard before. I think I must have been lapsing in and out of consciousness, because I would be in the middle of this maniacal abuse and then everything would go dark and quiet. Then I would come to and see his obscene face again and hear the horrific sounds and feel intense pain. I would cry and scream and he'd laugh and shove something else inside of me.

I don't know how long this went on for but when I finally woke from the nightmare, it was over and he was asleep on the rank and bloody bed beside me.

I crept to the door and tried it again, forgetting that I'd already found it locked. I heard a sound behind me and when I turned, he was standing there smiling and holding the key. Then a telephone rang in the kitchen. He went to answer it and I ran round looking for a means of escape, but nothing had changed. The heavy door was still locked and the only window was still boarded up.

His voice was placid on the phone, apologetic even. After a few minutes, he hung up and came to find me.

'That was my mother.'

I didn't answer, just backed away from him.

'I'm so sorry to have to leave you, Rozana. We had a wonderful time and I was hoping to spend the whole day with you.'

He seemed like a different person, as if the perverted events of the night before were perfectly normal to him. It was then I knew for sure that I had been abducted by an insane person – and I had to escape.

He began to get dressed in the clothes he was wearing in the bar and put on his glasses.

'But it's my birthday and my mother has planned a party.'

He took out a long length of thin chain from the bottom of his bedroom wardrobe and attached it to an iron bar that was fixed to the wall. He told me to sit on the bed while he handcuffed the other end of the chain to my right ankle.

When he left, I tested the extent of my freedom. I could reach the shower and toilet – there was a window high up in the wall, but it was too small to get through. I stood on the toilet seat and looked out. I guessed I was on the second or third floor of a building, but I didn't know what was above or below me. There were no other buildings nearby, just vacant land. I shouted and screamed for help, but no one responded, nor could I hear any other sounds coming from anywhere else in the building.

The chain allowed me to get to my clothes in the hallway, but not to the front door. In any case, I'm sure it would have been locked. I could get to some parts of the kitchen – a sofa and fridge and the sink for water, but not to the boarded window or the drawers where he probably kept the knife and other utensils that I might have used as weapons. There was no television or radio, just the CD player with his heavy metal music. Then the phone rang again – and I could reach it. I grabbed the receiver.

'Hello! Hello! Help me, please!'

'Rozana . . .'

It was Hugo.

'I just rang to say please help yourself to whatever you want from the fridge.'

He waited for my reply. An alien voice floated out of my mouth and hovered in the horrified air. Shivered. Shook.

'Thank you.'

'I'll see you later.'

I hung the phone up and immediately tried to dial the police, but he'd put a lock on the dialling disc. I could receive calls, but I couldn't ring out. I tried to get the lock off, but I had nothing to force it with. I was afraid to break the phone because, if I did and I still couldn't reach anyone, God knows what he would have done to me when he came back. I tried to undo the chain that attached me to the bar in the wall, but I couldn't. I screamed until I was hoarse, but nobody came.

When Hugo got back that evening, he brought me new clothes and unlocked the handcuffs from round my ankle. We had a takeaway to eat and he told me he lived with his mother, but he had a girlfriend to whom he was engaged.

'But I'll leave her, Rozana. I'll leave her and live with you forever.'

I didn't know if he meant his mother or his fiancé – and I didn't ask.

'You are the woman I have always dreamed of. I will give you everything. You will never have to want for anything.'

'I want to go home.'

'You *are* home, Rozana.'

'No, I'm not.'

He just smiled and shook his head and kissed my cheek.

That crazy bastard was a perfect gentleman during the day, but at night he turned into a perverted demon and, once again, I had to endure his sick fantasies for hours on end.

The next day he went out, leaving me chained up again. That evening, he brought another takeaway and flowers, and that's how the days and nights went by. I'd shower and try to soothe my damaged body, then sleep most of the day because I was kept awake most of the night. He'd come back in the evenings and bring me anything I asked for – before performing his unspeakable acts on me, as if I was a willing participant.

As the weeks went by, his sexual appetite became more and

more bizarre and perverse. He engaged in many sado-masochistic practises, tying me in various positions and inflicting pain before gratifying himself with an orgasm, either by means of sexual intercourse or masturbation. He even started dressing in women's underwear and made me penetrate him with a strap-on penis. At least this gave me relief from being constantly abused with all sorts of implements. During the days, I concentrated on small things – minutia – because the big thing of my captivity would have been too unbearable to contemplate.

I'd been a prisoner in that place for five weeks when he brought back some clothes in a dry-cleaner's bag. I assumed it was one of the suits he sometimes wore, or else some sex-role outfit.

The next morning, I went to the wardrobe to find something to wear and the bag was hanging there. I looked inside it and found a policeman's uniform. The uniform was not intended for any sex game and he took it away with him the next day. That's when I knew he could never let me leave alive and I realised I was not the first woman he'd held here.

I began to look for clues that might have been left by my predecessors. He obviously cleared the place out after every abduction, but I found a small set of initials, AR, carved into the kitchen wall. There were also some old bloodstains on the floor near the table and some long hairs behind the bed.

How many had there been before me?

I believed I'd stayed alive so long because of his changing sexual desires, but when he exhausted his repertoire and got bored, I'd be a dead woman. From then on, I kept suggesting variations on his disgusting routines, just to stay alive. I'm not proud of that now and it makes me sick to even think about it, but survival is the strongest human instinct and people in desperate situations will do desperate things.

Despite this, I knew it was only a matter of time before he killed me – I had to escape, there was no other option.

I'd been a prisoner for two months when the opportunity finally came. By this time Hugo had started to trust me and believed I actually enjoyed my time with him, so he stopped chaining me up when he went out during the day. The first time he did this, he waited outside the door for an hour and listened. I knew he was still there because I always heard his car starting in the mornings and that time it didn't. He came back in after an hour or so to see what I was up to, but I pretended to be asleep on the sofa. I did this for several days, because I didn't know if he was really gone or if he just drove down the road, testing me.

In the end, I had to take a chance because time was running out. I found the heavy knife he used to cut the pizza and I considered waiting until he came back and plunging it into his evil heart – but what if I couldn't? He was strong and I was weak – what if he took it away from me and plunged it into my own heart for betraying his trust? Even if I did manage to kill him, he was a policeman and they'd find me and the forensic evidence would be enough to convict me of murder – that is, if I ever got to trial.

So I started to cut away at the boards on the kitchen window. I knew he would see this when he came back, so I had to be gone by then. It took me most of the day and an ancient instinct kept me moving my arms – an energy that was beyond rage. Eventually, I managed to make a big enough hole to get through. I smashed the glass in the window and looked out. There was a ledge about halfway down, but too far to reach with my feet, even if I hung down by my arms from the window-sill. I'd have to drop onto it, then hang down from the ledge and drop to the ground. The ledge was only about a foot wide and, if I missed or lost my balance, Id fall the rest of the way and either be killed or seriously injured. But I'd be dead for sure if I stayed where I was, so there was really no choice.

I dressed in the clothes I'd been abducted in and left everything else there – then I climbed through the window, trying not to cut myself on the broken glass. I dropped my shoes and bag to the ground, thirty feet below, then I hung down as far as I could on the outside of the building. I'm a short person and even with my arms extended, there was still about six or seven feet between me and the ledge. I let go and felt my bare feet hit the concrete, and my knees take the force of the landing. I clasped the wall, scraping skin from my face and fingers, hoping the momentum of the drop wouldn't propel me backwards off the ledge. My toes gripped like claws and I steadied myself. I was alright, but there was still a further fifteen feet between me and the ground. I hung from the ledge and dropped the rest of the way down, this time onto the softer ground of the waste land.

I was free.

I saw that the place where I'd been kept prisoner was above an old abandoned warehouse. There were no other floors above and nothing below except a derelict goods shed. The building was away on its own, some distance from any others. It was an abductor's dream, and well prepared for unsuspecting women like me.

A new problem was knowing which direction to go. I had no clue regarding my whereabouts so I just ran towards the nearest road. I had some money still in my bag and I jumped onto the first bus that came along, not even knowing where it was going. Luckily, it was heading towards the city centre and I could find my way back to my flat from there.

It was getting dark by the time I reached home and I didn't even know what day it was. The first thing I did was get under my own shower and I stayed there for ages, until the water ran cold. Then I turned on the television and discovered it was Saturday. I would have Sunday to compose myself before I went back to work.

Work! It was the first time I'd even thought about it. I had been gone for two months. Where did they think I was? Had anyone notified the police? If so, they'd know where I lived. Were they looking for me? I hoped not. My abductor was a policeman and if they found me, they would surely kill me to protect him.

I began to panic. My flat wasn't safe, but there was nowhere else I could go. I locked the door, left all the lights off and hid under the bed, in case they came for me.

Thankfully, nobody did.

I didn't go out on Sunday, just kept a vigil by the window all day in case police cars pulled up in the street outside. If they did, my plan was to escape onto the roof and jump across to the next building, even if it meant risking a fall to my death.

Still, nobody came.

I lay in the bed that night, half asleep with one eye open, alert and startled by every small sound.

Quietly, anxiously, I waited for Monday to come.

CHAPTER SIXTEEN
ENGLAND

Monday came and I went to work, carefully checking out the building for parked police cars before entering. Most people didn't even realise I was missing because I travelled about so much, but my boss called me into his office.

'Rozana, where have you been?'

'I'm sorry. I became depressed after my father's death.'

'You should have called, Rozana!'

'I'm sorry. Did you . . . did you inform the police?'

'The police? What for? I knew you were at home with your family.'

What a relief! No police, but my boss was very disappointed that I had not called and, due to pressure from those above him, he was left with no choice but to demote me from National Merchandising Director to an ordinary salesperson, selling on the shop floor. I was back on the bottom rung of the ladder. Those two months away had cost me my job, and would also cost me my flat and my peace of mind, but what could I do? I couldn't go to the police and I was too ashamed to tell anyone else, considering the disgusting things I had been forced to do.

My greatest fear was AIDS. Could I have caught HIV from Hugo? I went to a doctor as soon as I was able and got myself tested. I waited in fear until the results came back, but they were clear. Even then, I was anxious and nervous every time I went out, in case someone was following me. I was terrified he would find me. I panicked every time I heard a siren or sensed someone behind me on the street. I kept away from quiet places and always stayed in the crowd.

I was also two months behind with my rent and, because of my demotion, I couldn't catch up. Eventually, I had to move to a cheaper flat that was further away from my work. One thing the abduction did teach me was to appreciate my life and freedom a lot more than I had ever done before. Strangely enough, I was much stronger emotionally. I realised that I didn't really want to die, despite the suicidal feelings I experienced in the depths of my depression. I promised myself I would never try to kill myself again, no matter how bad things got. Life was too precious and I had a lot of living I still needed to do.

I would be dead long enough.

My first assignment as an ordinary salesperson was in a small home improvements shop, selling the company's flooring products. It was owned by a woman called Tereza and we got on very well because we came from similar backgrounds. It was a family business and I helped her with stock control and customer care and all the other skills I had learned in the various jobs from over the years. In return, she let me sell whatever I liked and I made more commission than I would have by just selling the flooring products. My earnings soon went up and I was able to save some money.

It was November 1999 and I was approaching twenty-seven years of age. *Maximiliano Gaidzinsk S/A* began to deal with America and the company was sending selected staff abroad to learn English. My boss had always felt sorry for having to demote me and he asked if I would like him to put my name forward. The company would pay for the course, but I would have to find the money for the flight and for living expenses while I was away. I'd never even considered leaving Brazil before, but I saw it as a chance to get away from the threat of Hugo finding me again and I accepted his offer immediately.

I couldn't get a visa to travel to America because I had no connections there, neither had I any money in the bank and no family in São Paulo to give me references – and I could not apply again for six months. I didn't want to wait that long. There were courses available in England, but there was a chance I would be turned down for a visa there too. I spoke to Tereza about it and she said it was too good an opportunity to miss. She recommended I talk to one of the salespeople in the shop, a girl called Nisi.

Nisi was a friendly girl in her mid-twenties and she was intending to go abroad as an au-pair.

'Do you know how I can get an English visa, Nisi?'

'Yes, just register as an au-pair with an agency.'

She told me many British families were looking for experienced child-minders and the agency would get me a visa and a job. This seemed ideal to me, as it would provide me with enough money to live on while I was studying English on my course. So I registered with the M-Brazil Agency that had an office in São Paulo. They had connections with the Samuel Brown au-pair agency in England.

When I left the job with *Maximiliano Gaidzinsk S/A*, I signed a contract to be re-employed by them when I came back. I was paid a good deal of money in what we Brazilian's call *Fundo de Garantia*, which is a worker guarantee payment deducted from your wages and returned to you when you leave that employment. I put this with my savings, but I still had to borrow money from my friend Malu, from the salons, to pay M-Brazil four thousand American dollars. They gave me a telephone number and I called the Samuel Brown Agency in England. I was able to talk to them with the aid of a friend who spoke English.

'What should I do?'

'Just come. We'll sort everything out when you get here.'

Nisi decided to travel with me and we bought two return tickets for one thousand two hundred American dollars each. That was all the money I had – there was nothing left, and I owed Malu money that I promised to pay back as soon as I could. The tickets gave us up to a year to take a course and make the return journey. But a week before we were due to leave, we discovered there was no such thing as an au-pair visa for Brazilians – it seemed the M-Brazil Agency had lied to us. I couldn't back out though because I already had my ticket and arranged with the company to take a year's unpaid sabbatical to learn English and to bring my new language back to work for them. I'd signed a contract and they had given me £950 to pay for the course, which I was supposed to do when I got to England.

Nisi and I flew out of Guarulhos International Airport en route to Schipol International Airport in Holland. The flight was eleven hours long and we had to catch another flight from there to England. I arrived at Heathrow airport at 3:45pm on 16th January, 2000, with no visa, no English skills and no idea of where I was going or what I was doing.

The Samuel Brown Agency told us that two English families would be waiting for us and everything would be sorted out quickly. As excited as I was, it was still terrifying to arrive in a country on the other side of the equator with no knowledge of the language, the currency, the customs or climate. I intended to find a language school and book my course and then apply for a student visa. If I could not get a student visa, I would have to change my flight dates and go home empty handed.

We only had Brazilian passports, so we told immigration we were tourists on vacation. Nisi got through quicker than me because she had an address that was given to her by the agency. I did not. I had no credit cards or any other identification, other than my passport. I had nowhere to go – no address and no hotel – and I didn't know anyone in England. I felt sure they wouldn't let me in, but I tried to convince them I was a backpacker and I'd find a cheap hostel to stay in. I think the fact that Nisi was my friend and that she had an address finally won them over, so they gave me a tourist visa for six months and let me through.

Nisi was waiting for me outside, but there was no one there waiting for us like the agency had promised. About half an hour later, a black woman called Ola rushed in, apologising for being late, and she took Nisi away with her. I waited for more than four hours, but nobody came for me. I was resigned to sleeping at the airport and going back to Brazil on the first available flight the next day. But at around 8:00pm, a woman with a heavy African accent came over, carrying a piece of cardboard with my name on it. I couldn't understand a word she said, but I made out that her name was Olivia and I was to go with her.

The Samuel Brown Agency told me I would be looking after two white English children and they even sent me pictures of the family and the lovely house they lived in. The reality was very different. Olivia took me to a house in Leyton, East London, where she had six very noisy children between the ages of four and seventeen. The house was a slum, dark and dismal with no gas or electricity – there was no furniture either. The bathroom was falling down and smelled horrible and the kitchen was dirty and greasy. It looked like a kind of halfway house, where people might only stay for a short while, before being moved on to somewhere else. The building was crawling with rats – if anything dropped on the floor, the rodents would run out and eat it. The children were unwashed and slept on bare mattresses. They didn't go to school and they were constantly shouting and swearing and fighting.

Olivia showed me to my room, which was small and smelled of mould and urine. It had a single bed and a shelf, nothing else, and a grimy window that looked out over a back garden full of high weeds. I'd lived in many disgusting and frightening places, so it was nothing new to me, but I'd paid the M-Brazil Agency four thousand dollars, which was a lot of money to me, and I expected something better. I was very tired after my long journey, but it was difficult to sleep with the noise of the children and the rats scurrying round under my bed.

I had arrived on a Sunday and I got up early the following morning, expecting Olivia to go to work, but she just hung round the house drinking and smoking all day. I tried to communicate with the children as best I could, I had a Portuguese to English dictionary and if I couldn't pronounce the word I wanted to say, I would just point to it and they'd read it. I had no specific duties as such, Olivia just seemed to want someone to be there with the children when she went out, and she went out a lot. I wasn't happy with the situation, but I told myself the best thing I could do was get on with it.

There was no food in the house and I had to go buy milk and bread with my own money. As soon as I got back, the children mobbed me like starving cats and anything that dropped on the floor was devoured in seconds by the rats.

Olivia had an Afro-Caribbean boyfriend who was a Bob Marley lookalike, with dreadlocks and gold teeth. She would disappear for days at a time with him and I would be left alone with the children. The M-Brazil Agency told me I'd be paid £50 a week, through my employer, but I never received any money in all the time I was there. Whenever I asked Olivia for my wages, she made the excuse that her "payment" was late. I don't know what kind of payment she meant, maybe benefits, but it never came and I never got paid.

After a couple of weeks, when I found my feet a bit, I called Nisi from a public payphone. It was the first time I'd spoken to her since she left me at Heathrow Airport and it was really good to hear a voice I understood. We had a long chat and I told her something wasn't right about the Samuel Brown Agency. I believed they were smuggling in illegal immigrants, but she was with a nice family in Epping Forest who were paying her and treating her well – so maybe I was just imagining things. We agreed to meet up the following weekend and I couldn't wait to see her.

Olivia went out when I got back and left me with the children, as usual. I thought she was with her boyfriend, but he came round on his own with pizza for the kids. He spoke to me and made gestures, indicating that he wanted me to go somewhere with him.

With the help of my dictionary, I worked out that he was saying I had to go with him to get electricity. I didn't know how you could buy electricity and bring it back to the house – like in a bag or something? I started laughing and this made him angry. He showed me a card and said something else I did not understand. I tried to speak English in a broken accent.

'What . . . about . . . children?'

'They'll be okay. We'll only be a few minutes.'

We walked through many back streets until we came to a house where a group of people were sniffing ketamine and smoking cannabis. Olivia's boyfriend tried to get me to sniff some of the powder, but I refused. I told him I wanted to leave and he said he'd walk me back. When we passed a public telephone, I went in and closed the door, but he came into the box after me and started touching me. I called Nisi and she told me to get him to take me to a bar, somewhere close to where I was living, and then run away from him. I smiled at him and made a drinking sign.

He smiled back.

We went to a bar called The Red Lion and I bought two drinks. He sat at a table and I indicated that I had to go to the toilet. As soon as I was away from him, I ran out of the bar and back to Olivia's house. He came after me and was banging on the door, but I wouldn't let him in.

'Open the door, you bitch!'

'Polícia! Polícia!'

I made out I was calling the police. There was no phone in the house so it wasn't possible, but the threat must have been enough because he went away.

All this time, I should have been on a course studying English. The agency was supposed to help me find a language school and enrol, but they did nothing for me. I wasn't getting paid either and I was spending the money *Maximiliano Gaidzinsk S/A* gave me to pay for my lessons.

On the Wednesday before I was due to meet Nisi, Olivia left the house and took all the children with her. She said something to me before she went, but I couldn't understand it. She wrote a number on a piece of paper, but I didn't understand that either. I thought she was just going out somewhere for the day, but evening came and she didn't return.

It got dark and there was no gas or electricity and the rats were scurrying around and squeaking. She didn't come back the next day either. It was winter and I had never experienced cold dark-rainy days like that before. I was freezing and there was no way to heat the house, so the only way to keep warm was to stay in bed, fully clothed. I had no contact details for the Samuel Brown Agency – no address or location, just the telephone number M-Brazil gave me back in Sao Paulo. When I called it, I got the operator saying I had a wrong number.

On the Friday, I went out and called the number on the piece of paper Olivia had given me. I took my dictionary with me, but my hands were so cold that I dialled the wrong number. A voice answered in Portuguese.

'Olá.'

'Hello.'

'Quem é?'

I answered in Portuguese.

'Você fala português?'

'Falo, brasileira.'

Was this coincidence or was it fate? She told me her name was Abigail and she had only been in London for a week. She and her friend, Fabian, were au-pairs, recruited by the Samuel Brown Agency, and they were living in slums with very poor families. We spoke for a while and I told her I was meeting up with my friend, Nisi, and it would be great if all four of us could get together. I took some food back to the cold house and I ate it before going inside, because the rats would swarm around me if they smelled it, climbing all over me and sitting on my shoulders like squirrels. It was hard staying in that cold dark house with only the rodents for company.

Nobody came by and I never saw Olivia or her children again.

When Saturday arrived, I was nervous about using the underground for the first time. But I'd managed it in São Paulo when I went there and Nisi had explained to me how to get to Liverpool Street station by just going four stops west on the Central Line. This was where we had all agreed to meet before travelling on together to the West End.

Nisi arrived and it was so wonderful to meet someone from Brazil after all those dark days alone. We were so excited to see each other again. Then Abigail arrived. She was twenty-two and tall and beautiful, with a bright smile – and I knew immediately it was her, without ever seeing her before.

'Hello! I'm Abigail.'

'I'm Rozana. This is Nisi.'

We all hugged each other like we were sisters, then I noticed a shy, dark-haired twenty-two-year-old girl with beautiful blue eyes standing behind Abigail, who introduced her as Fabian. We had so much to say to each other and we stood there talking for almost an hour, blocking the flow of people coming up the escalators. I knew from that moment on we would be friends forever – me and Nisi and Abi and Fabi, as we called our two new friends from then on.

I couldn't face going back to the empty rat-house so, after our day of exploring central London, Nisi took me back with her to Epping Forest. The woman she worked for was kind and she found me a job as an au-pair with a family in Dagenham.

It was another African family and they had two sweet children aged five and two. The mother was a teacher and the father worked shifts at the car factory. They were very nice people, but they were very religious and had strict rules. They dressed in traditional African clothes on Sundays and went to church. They also had a tight work regime, with certain days set aside for washing and ironing, and everything was done to a methodical and regulated routine.

I was only paid £40 for a six-day week. I sent £10 to my mother in Brazil and put £20 into a bank account so I could prove to the Home Office I had enough money to live on for six months and they'd give me a student visa. That left me with £10 to spend on the Saturdays I had off to meet with my friends. We would start with breakfast at McDonald's in Liverpool Street and stay there until the bars opened. Then we would tour round central London, drinking cheap, low-alcohol beer. They weren't really bar-crawls, they were just fun days out, exploring and going to free museums and exhibitions. None of us had a lot of money so we only went places we could get in for free. We would laugh together and make the drinks last a long time.

One of the rules of my new home in Dagenham was, if I wasn't back by 10:00pm on Saturday night, the house would be locked up and I couldn't get in until 8:00am Sunday morning. I was never back on time. We would go to a nightclub before 10:00pm so we could get in for free, then we would dance all night until three or four in the morning. We'd make our way to Leicester Square tube station after the clubs closed and wait for the first trains to take us home. We had many individual challenges to face. Nisi and I were with decent families, but Abi and Fabi still lived in slums. Still, we were having the time of our lives! A group of young Brazilian women in their mid-twenties, living in London for the first time – it was a dream.

I still hadn't managed to enrol in a language school because the people I worked for wouldn't give me the time off, but I was picking up a little more English every day. My duties as an au-pair were, taking the children to school and nursery, cleaning the house and, after school, taking the children to the local park.

The weeks went by and, in the Spring of 2000, I came across the most beautiful man I had ever seen in my life. It was an afternoon in April and I was in the park with the children. He was in his late twenties and blonde with blue eyes. I immediately forgot about all the other men I had been in love with over the years – the ones I thought I had been in love with. I couldn't take my eyes off him and he noticed me staring. He had a young girl of about six with him who was very pretty and I stayed in the park for two hours, much longer than I ever had before – waiting until he left, without speaking to me.

I went back to the park every afternoon that week.

But he wasn't there.

CHAPTER SEVENTEEN
LOVE

I began going to the park in the evenings, when the children went to bed, and staying there until it got dark.

Still there was no sign of the blonde man.

It seemed as if he'd vanished and I began to wonder if I'd just imagined him. Was he a ghost, with his cautious step and enigmatic expression and his nymph-like little companion?

Then, one evening, I left the park to go home when the light began to fade. As I was waiting to cross a road, I saw him on the other side. I didn't want to miss this opportunity to find out if he was real, or an *espírito*. God only knew if and when I might see him again, so I hurried across and "accidentally" bumped into him. My English was very poor, but I tried to have a conversation.

'Hello.'

'Oh, hello.'

'I saw you in the park.'

'I remember.'

'Who is the little girl?'

'My daughter.'

He was real.

He had a Scottish accent and I had a Brazilian accent, and we communicated as best we could in English. He told me his name was Alex and asked if I would like to meet up on my day off. I always went into London with the girls on Saturday, but this week they would have to go without me.

I couldn't understand what time Alex said to meet him, so to be on the safe side, I went to the park at 10:00am. There was no sign of him and I waited for hours. I was about to give up and go join my friends when I saw the little six-year-old girl coming through the gate. He followed her, wearing a yellow T-shirt and jeans and a baseball cap. It was 2:00pm. Alex introduced his daughter as Gemma. She had blonde hair like her father and the bluest eyes I had ever seen, as blue as the sky. She went to play while we tried to have a conversation.

We talked a bit about ourselves and Alex told me he had split up from Gemma's mother a short time ago. He saw his daughter once a week and usually took her to the park, if the weather was good. It was very difficult for me to understand what he was saying and I'm sure it must have been just as hard for him to understand me, but I gathered that he was devastated over the break-up with Gemma's mother, who he called Sharon. He started to cry while he was talking about her, so I quickly changed the subject. I told him I was from Brazil and I'd come over to learn English, but I had to take a job as an au-pair to earn money. He said he was an engineer working for Thames Water and he had a flat there in Dagenham. I wondered if he was still in love with this Sharon woman – if he was, I'd probably be wasting my time, but he asked if he could see me again and I agreed.

We met in the park almost every evening over the next few days – just on our own, without Gemma or the children I was looking after. He began to open up to me about his relationship with Sharon in a way that was a little disconcerting. I was a relative stranger – an alien, from a different set of circumstances. Did he not have friends he could confide in? He told me she had run off with someone else. He loved her and did everything for her, but she was a bitch and she slept with this other man behind his back. He painted a bad picture of Sharon and I didn't care much for her and I felt sorry for him, despite my trepidation. I told him I didn't have a husband or a boyfriend, but I went into London every Saturday with my friends and had a good time.

Despite our different backgrounds, we related well with each other, Alex and I. We were both damaged and trying to put ourselves back together and, if talking to each other could help that healing process, then it could only be a good thing.

As time went by, I realised Alex had mood issues. He became agitated sometimes and swore a lot and occasionally passed nasty comments on people in the street. Other times he got angry with me if I expressed an opinion he didn't agree with and it seemed as if he was sporadically and intermittently irritated by everything around him. He wasn't physically violent and I assumed his chagrin was because Sharon was giving him a lot of problems. He told me she wouldn't leave him alone and it was "doing his head in". But he had the ability to fold his pique into a flower and I was falling in love with him and Gemma and would take their side against anyone, especially a bad woman like Sharon.

Sharon and Alex were never married, they just lived together for eight years, so there was no nasty divorce or anything like that. I wondered what kind of problems she could be causing for him.

Spring turned to Summer and Alex and I continued our platonic relationship, meeting in the park either on our own or with the children. My English was improving all the time and we were now able to communicate reasonably well. One day he surprised me –

'Do you like your job, Rozana?'

'It's alright. I will be going back to Brazil next year.'

'Do you want to go back to Brazil?'

'My real job is there.'

'But, do you want to go back?'

It was the first time I'd thought about going back, and I had mixed feelings about it. After the initial shock of living with Olivia, I was liking my stay in London, but I wasn't getting any younger and I didn't want to spend the rest of my life as an au-pair. He sensed my hesitancy.

'You could move in with me, then you could work at whatever

you want.'

By the end of the Summer, we were living together.

Once I moved in with Alex, I was able to apply for my student visa, which only allowed me to work twenty hours a week, and I started an English course at the London Skills Institute. I also got a job as a waitress at The London Eye, working for Costa Coffee Events Department – me and a German guy called Rick. We served champagne and canapés to millionaires and married couples and I loved it! It was good fun. The wheel took twenty-four minutes to go round and we would do four events in a day, one after the other. I got great tips and learned a lot about event catering.

I did this job in the mornings and went to my English course at The London Skills Institute in the afternoons. The course cost £480 for a year, which was less than the £950 *Maximiliano Gaidzinsk S/A* gave me, but I had spent most of the rest by then, so it was just as well.

Alex was wonderful to me – he cooked breakfast for me and drove me to work and bought me flowers. I loved him so much. He did things no other man had ever done for me and he was a gentle and caring lover. I was now sure of what I wanted to do – I wanted to stay in England with Alex, so I phoned my boss at *Maximiliano Gaidzinsk S/A* and asked him if I could end my contract with the company.

'But why, Rozana?'

'I've met someone over here. I'm in love!'

He was very understanding and wished me luck with my new life, but I think he was still feeling sorry for having to demote me and this was his way of making it up to me.

'I will pay back the money you gave me for the course.'

'There's no need for that, Rozana.'

'Really?'

'Consider it to be a wedding present.'

I was so happy. My life was beginning to have meaning. The sun was shining for me at last.

It was in the Autumn that Alex dropped the bombshell.

'Listen, Rozana. I want Sharon and Gemma to move in with us.'

'What?'

'Just hear me out, please . . .'

They lost their house when they split up and Sharon moved in with a friend. Gemma was sleeping on the floor and now the friend wanted them out. He had offered to take Gemma in, but the girl wouldn't come without her mother.

'It'll just be temporary, until they find somewhere.'

'There's no room.'

'Yes there is. The flat's big enough. They can have one bedroom and we'll have the other.'

'Why can't she go to her family?'

'She comes from a troubled background. I can't send her back there, especially with Gemma.'

What could I say? It was his flat and I loved Gemma so much and couldn't bear the thought of her being homeless with Winter coming. So I succumbed.

Sharon was tall, unlike me, with dark hair and blue eyes. She was very slim and, right from the start, I didn't like her – so we rarely spoke.

Alex worked long hours – he'd leave home at 5:00am and sometimes not come home until 8:00pm. Then they would be in the living room together, like a family, and I felt left out. It was very hard for me to accept Sharon in the flat and Alex and I were constantly rowing about it. He would give me funny looks if I joined them in the evening, so I started staying in the bedroom. This didn't please him either and he accused me of snubbing them.

My friends told me I should leave, but I had nowhere else to go. I was only earning £120 a week and I had to pay travel fares and my share of the rent. As well as that, I was trying to save a bit so I could prove to the Home Office I had enough to live on, in order to renew my student visa for a further six months. So, there was nothing left – certainly not enough to rent a place of my own in London.

Sharon and Gemma moved out after about a month. I don't know where they went and I was glad to see them go, but things between myself and Alex didn't improve. He seemed to be angry a lot of the time and I was unsure why. Some days I dreaded him coming home. I'm not saying he was violent, but there was a constant undercurrent of tension and discontent and it felt like he was a human volcano that could erupt at any time.

Once, he came in angry and said he saw Sharon with a man. He was shouting and swearing and I couldn't understand why this would make him so angry. I decided to ring my boss again at *Maximiliano Gaidzinsk S/A* and tell him I had made a mistake and ask if I could have my job back after I finished the English course.

'Of course you can, Rozana.'

That gave me peace of mind, because I knew my situation in London was now temporary and I would be going back to Brazil. I loved Alex, but living with him was getting too hard – too volatile.

One day, Sharon came to the door while he was at work.

'What do you want?'

'To talk.'

I didn't have a good opinion of Sharon from the things Alex had said about her, but I let her in and we talked. She came across as a caring person and not insecure at all, like he said she was. She told me he was following her everywhere and telling her he loved her. Instead of going to work, sometimes he parked his van outside her house and waited for her to come out. She hoped when he met me, he would leave her alone, but he didn't and she couldn't cope any more.

'Why did you came back here, Sharon, if you knew it might cause these problems?'

'I had nowhere else to go.'

'Why are you telling me this now? Why have you come here?'

'I don't know. Maybe you could do something about it?'

'Like what?'

'I don't know!'

I wasn't sure whether to believe her or not. I confronted Alex when he came home and he said she was lying. He became angry and said he didn't think our relationship was working out and he wanted me to leave his flat. I was glad in a way – relieved, even though I had no place to go. I phoned the girls and, luckily, Abigail and Fabian had left their slum au-pair jobs and were now sharing a flat in Tooting Broadway, south-east London. They said I could go and stay with them.

I was glad to have found a place to stay so quickly, but all the girls had steady boyfriends and were with them most of the time. Our days of exploring London together were over and I felt like an outsider. I missed Alex as well, despite everything – and Gemma. The thought that I would never see either of them again made me feel sad and very lonely – and I worried in case the old depression returned.

Then Alex sent me a text message, saying he made a mistake asking me to leave. He was under a lot of pressure – he was sorry and wanted me back. The girls said I would be crazy to go back to him, but I couldn't think straight because I missed him so much.

I decided to give our relationship another chance. I met him the following weekend and told him we could see each other again, but I didn't want to move back into his flat because I was going back to Brazil when my course finished. He seemed kinder, not so irritated all the time – not so on edge, like he had been. We were great together and it was like when we first met, perhaps even better.

Things were perfect again.

It was December and Alex asked me to go to Scotland with him for Christmas, to meet his parents. Before we went, he gave me a ring and asked me to marry him. I didn't know what to say, it was such a shock and I was overwhelmed. To be married to a man I loved and have a nice house and a family was always my ultimate dream – but it would mean not going back to Brazil and many other things besides.

My mind was whirling.

After I composed myself, we had a long conversation and I said I had to be certain he loved me and not Sharon. I'd changed my mind twice about going back to Brazil and, if I did it again, I wanted it to be the last time. He assured me that he loved me unconditionally and I believed him. I wanted to believe him so much. My dream was coming true. I would belong somewhere – with someone – and life would be perfect at last.

We went to Scotland that Christmas and it snowed. It was the first time I had ever seen snow and it was like a fairyland; a fairytale. The daytime light was full of secrets and at night the sky was sprinkled with stars that sparkled on the snow like dancing fire-flies, while the ghost of a moon smiled down and said "welcome." I knew then all that mattered was the here and now. Nothing had gone before and nothing would follow. And I understood what the old Shamen said, that contentment is a place that lies hidden in the heart and the journey there is a spiritual one – across doubts and fears and difficulties.

Alex's mother and stepfather lived in Glasgow with his two teenage sisters. They were very welcoming and friendly and we stayed there for four days. When we got back, I contacted *Maximiliano Gaidzinsk S/A* again. I felt so bad – so ungrateful for all my boss had done for me there. I kept changing my mind and he'd been so understanding about what was happening to me. It would seem that I was indecisive and unthankful – but I wasn't, I really appreciated his patience. It was just that my life seemed to be a rollercoaster of emotion and I didn't know when I'd be able to get off the ride.

Again, I told him what was happening.

Again, he understood.

I didn't re-book my return flight so when the date to depart came and went, I lost my seat. That was it, I had burned all my bridges and there was no going back.

We booked the wedding for 15th July, 2001, and I thought things couldn't get any better. Then, two months before we were due to get married, I found out I was pregnant. Alex and I never talked about having children and I was a bit concerned as to what his reaction would be, but I need not have worried because he was absolutely delighted.

Our wedding took place on a lovely Summer's day in a beautiful part of the Scottish countryside. We were married in a three-hundred-year-old registry office and Gemma was my bridesmaid. We had a family lunch for twenty people, followed by a reception at a hotel with a hundred guests, including my friends from London.

We went to the island of Iona on our honeymoon, across the sound on a boat. I fell in love with the place as we drove through its bays and beaches and explored its islets and skerries, spending a week of long, hazy days together. Alex made me feel loved like I never imagined I would be. It was wonderful – a wonderland – and I never thought about Brazil or London or the rest of the world for a single second.

When it was over, we went back to the flat in Dagenham and our life as a married couple began. We were happy – Gemma would come at weekends and we would go for walks together. Alex was a loving, attentive husband and I was a blissful, heavily pregnant wife during that long, latent summer.

Labour was hell and I passed out every time I had a contraction. At one point I believed I was dead and could see myself in the bed, but it wasn't really me. Alex was trying to comfort me and my head was on his shoulder. I was trying to tell him I was dead and there would be no baby and no more me. Then I was back in the pain again and I believed I'd carry the agony for eternity because of all the sins I'd committed. They gave me epidurals, but they didn't work.

After fifteen hours, a nurse realised I hadn't dilated and there was no way the baby could be born – we could both die. The baby was as distressed as I was and, eventually, they gave me an emergency caesarean section under general anaesthetic.

At 3:15pm on Monday, 1st October, 2001, our beautiful daughter Julia was born and when I woke up, Alex was holding her in his arms. But I was so ill I couldn't take her from him. They were making me breastfeed but I couldn't. I was shaking and had no feeling in any part of my body. A nurse told me I had to hold Julia because she needed contact with her mother. I held her on my chest and fell asleep.

When I awoke, the pain was back. This time it was caused by an infection after the operation. I was ill for the next few days and was finding it very hard to bond with Julia. I couldn't even hold her in my arms and I felt that having her was a mistake.

I stayed in the hospital for a week and when it was time to go home, I started having panic attacks. I just didn't know how I was going to take care of a baby when I wasn't even confident in taking care of myself. I felt like a monster.

How can a mother not love her new-born baby?

This wasn't how it was supposed to be – not at all! Every time I held Julia I burst into tears and my whole body shivered like I was going to die. I was physically and emotionally traumatised.

That's when I began to lose my memory – or part of my memory. I used to forget I had a baby and I would sometimes leave her in shops and in the park. I'd make coffee and forget about it and realise I made it six hours later. I would forget about food cooking and burn it. When I went to sleep, I believed I was dying – for months I believed I was going to die at any moment. I was having panic attacks and shaking and my heart would beat abnormally fast. I felt so guilty – my dream had come true and I was wrecking it. I should be so happy and not behaving like a neurotic, psychotic, crazy person. It must have been hell for Alex too, trying to cope with me. And he did his best – no man could have done more. But gradually, the old angry Alex re-surfaced.

And then it got worse.

Sharon lost the house she was living in and was on the street. Alex decided that Gemma had to come live with us full-time until her mother could find another place. The news was like a bucket of cold water being poured over my head. Although I loved Gemma dearly, I was barely holding onto my sanity. I couldn't cope with myself and my baby, how could I cope with a seven-year-old child as well?

It wasn't the beginning of the end for Alex and me – it was the end of the beginning.

CHAPTER EIGHTEEN
LOSS

The first week home was the most difficult. I couldn't eat or sleep properly. Alex was still working long hours and wasn't there to support me. I blamed him for not being there for me, but it wasn't really his fault – there was no paternity leave then and he had to work to support us.

After the caesarean section, I shouldn't have been lifting anything, but I had to get Julia's pram up and down flights of stairs and do all the normal housekeeping tasks like cooking, cleaning, washing and making beds. It seemed to me like I was in some kind of perpetual bad dream.

We lived in a rough area and I seemed to be able to hear every sound from the streets outside our windows – fights and shouts and screams and glass breaking. I would hear everything in a surreal way – half awake and half asleep – in a twilight state, not knowing whether it was imagined or not. I had the taste of blood in my mouth for months and I cried constantly, thinking I was going to die. I don't know why.

When Gemma came to live with us, it got even harder. I had to bring her to school in the cold winter, make sure she had clean clothes and take care of all her young seven-year-old problems, along with minding myself and the baby. Gemma was sweet and caring but, to be honest, the last thing I needed then was the responsibility of looking after her.

Fabi came round as much as possible to help me, and my mother-in-law visited her granddaughter from Scotland. I tried to hide my despondency as much as I could and nobody really knew the extent of my trauma. Alex did his best, but he just didn't understand. In fact, he knew very little about me – not even the small things, like my favourite colour. I was desperate to talk to him – really talk to him – to try to explain what was wrong with me, even though I wasn't sure myself. But he was tired when he came in from work and his weekends were preoccupied with Gemma and Julia.

Alex was never an easy man to get close to – I mean, really close to. He was caring and considerate and I loved him, but he always held a bit of himself back. He kept a part of himself to himself and was not interested in the very intimate knowing of each other that real marriage means – being able to tell what the other person is thinking and feeling. He tried to solve problems he didn't understand with money. I could have whatever I wanted, spend whatever I wanted. He substituted money for that special kind of attention only a few men know how to provide, and it wasn't really his fault. I know that now, even though I didn't realise it then.

I was impossible to live with and Alex had other problems, both work related and personal, that I didn't know about. So, he dealt with the difficulties in the only way he knew how. I tried to show him that money didn't matter to me by tearing it up in front of him, but he would just walk away.

I want to make it absolutely clear that I am not blaming Alex for the early deterioration of our marriage. No normal man could have put up with me after Julia was born. Even before she came into the world, I didn't really have a high sex drive, probably because of the way I was abused over the years. After the baby was born, I didn't want sex at all. This was an added difficulty for Alex to deal with – it would have been for any man. But I felt nothing at all. I had no libido left.

In the beginning, he said it didn't matter. But after about six months, he began to get frustrated with my excuses to keep him away from me – they weren't convincing anymore. My doctor sent me to a sex therapist because my hormones were completely messed up – but I think the therapist needed help herself, because she was half asleep all the time. I was booked for ten sessions, but I stopped going after four. The only good thing was, after a few months, I finally began to love Julia as I should have done from the moment she was born. However, when I remembered the actual birth, my whole body still shook and the sensation of dying returned.

Because I was breastfeeding and was not having sex, I didn't bother to take a contraceptive pill. So the first time Alex and I made love after Julia was born, I became pregnant again. When I found out, I almost had a nervous breakdown – I was absolutely traumatised. The doctor offered me an abortion because I got so sick having Julia, but I believe life begins at the moment of conception and I couldn't go through with it. I was having terrible nightmares, dreaming I was in labour, and I'd wake up crying, with actual labour pains. Even though I refused a termination, there were many times when I wished I would lose the child naturally. I hated myself for having those thoughts, but I couldn't help it. I felt so guilty because, deep down, I really didn't want this baby and I believed the negativity inside me might cause all kinds of abnormalities.

As I said, where we lived in Dagenham was a rough area and Alex decided we should move out of London because it would be better for the children – but not so far out that he'd have to travel a long distance to work. We found a two-bedroom flat in Hoddesdon, Hertfordshire. It was nice and quiet there and the flat had a balcony overlooking a green area. Alex also got custody of Gemma when we moved to Hoddesdon and Sharon had her on weekends.

After three months of pregnancy, my first scan was booked. I slept badly the night before and I kept dreaming the baby wasn't there anymore. In the morning, I felt tired and not very well as I took Gemma to school. When I got back to the flat, I went to the toilet and noticed that I was bleeding. I rang my doctor and he advised me to see him before I went for the scan. On the way down to the surgery, I felt very dizzy and I passed out. I don't know how long I was on the ground, but when I came to, I was lying in a huge pool of blood and Julia was still asleep in her pushchair.

Nobody came to help me.

I panicked and rushed straight to the doctor's surgery. They put me in an ambulance and took me to the hospital. They performed the scan and, just like in my dream the night before, the baby wasn't there.

I had such mixed feelings about it – on the one hand, I blamed myself for the miscarriage, for wishing it. On the other hand, I was utterly relieved.

I believe that, most times, you can take control of your life, but occasionally some things are meant to be and there is nothing you can do to alter the outcome.

I stayed in the hospital overnight and when I was leaving the next day, I spoke to a senior nurse about my fear of having another baby. She advised me to put Julia on a bottle and use contraceptives, which I did straight away. I also spoke to her about my aversion to sex and she said this was normal after having such a difficult labour and a complicated birth. She spoke to Alex too and he was quite understanding. He avoided me as much as he could and we probably only had sex about three times over the next six months. Every time we did make love, I believed I was going to get pregnant and, sure enough, despite being on the contraceptives, I became pregnant again. It must have been mind over matter – the state of my mind over the matter of the contraceptives. Whatever it was, it caused calamity.

At the same time, I got a letter from Brazil saying my brother Manoel had been killed. I asked Alex if I could go back for the funeral and he agreed. I took Julia with me and Gemma stayed with Alex.

Manoel had lost a finger operating farm machinery when he was twelve, so he went to work as a waiter and saved his tips. Manoel was very good at making money. He bought a share in a bar and sold it for a good profit. Then he borrowed money from banks at low interest and loaned it out at high interest. He used some of the money he made to improve our family's lifestyle. He also bought a powerful motorbike and was killed in a crash on the *Rodovia Regis Bittencourt*. The ironic thing was, the people who owed him money decided it no longer had to be paid back, but the banks he owed money to decided it did.

My family had a television now and everyone was watching Brazilian soaps. It brought another dimension into their lives – another perspective – and they could see there was life beyond Lageado. Living in England gave me a certain status and they were more respectful towards me than the last time I visited.

While I was there, I told my sister Celia that I was pregnant and about my fear of labour and childbirth. She made me a brew of some kind of tea mixture that she said would abort the baby I was carrying. I put it to my lips, but I couldn't force myself to drink it. That's when something strange happened and everything changed. I started to feel completely different. For some reason, it felt right. I cannot explain why my attitude changed, it was a kind of spiritual thing – an ineffable watershed. Like some mystical thing had entered me and was soothing away all my anxieties. A calmness came over me and I felt at ease with my pregnancy. Even though I'd had a miscarriage not that long before and Julia was only eighteen-months-old, I felt ready to have another child. This new serenity kept me happy with my family for the two weeks I stayed in Lageado but, as always, I was glad to leave when the time came.

I went into labour in January, 2004. Alex took me to the hospital and the doctor said everything was normal, but I should go home, as they baby would not be born for quite a while yet. I somehow knew he was wrong and that the baby would come soon.

I was right.

Three hours later I was ready to give birth. However, just as before, I hadn't dilated and had to be given a caesarean section. It was nothing like the previous time, no complications or infections, and I was completely calm throughout the procedure.

Alex and I thought I was having another girl and we were both happy about it once I'd overcome my phobia. We thought it would be good for Julia to have a little sister. But to our surprise, on 14th January after three hours in labour and a caesarean, baby Callum was born. He was a gorgeous little boy and I loved him from the start. Both Gemma and Julia were delighted to have a little brother and Alex had always wanted a son, so he was happy too. I remember coming back from the hospital with Callum and he said to me –

'The only thing we need to make life perfect is our own house.'

I knew he meant it.

Alex was a very hard worker, he started doing all the hours he could to bring home as much money as possible, so we could afford a down payment on a mortgage. I had an Argentinean neighbour called Veronica who was a doctor, specialising in diabetes, and married to a scientist. She'd had a baby and gave up working and was struggling on her husband's wages. We came to an arrangement – I paid her to look after the children and I went out to work full-time, cleaning offices for a contract company, to help with the mortgage deposit.

Somebody once said, "When you desire something, all the universe conspires in helping you to achieve it," that is if the desire is good and originates in the soul of the universe. I'm not sure if this is true or not, because desire tends to destroy and the rich parts of this world are steeped in the culture of want these days. However, Alex was working on an underground tunnel to put treated water into the Thames, when he and his team found some old Victorian copper pipes that were worth a lot of money. His share of the reward was £15,000 and suddenly, unexpectedly, we had enough for our deposit.

By the time baby Callum was four months old, we had moved

into our new Hertfordshire home. We believed we had everything we needed and it was a happy time.

During the first year, we furnished our house, planted the garden and installed a new kitchen. Once that was done, I began saving so we could all go to Brazil. I wanted my family to meet Alex and the children and I wanted Alex and the children to meet my family. We went there in July 2005, when the weather was cooler than in the steamy Summer. We spent some time in Lageado and travelled round sightseeing and taking the children to the beach. It was a wonderful time. Alex seemed really happy. He fitted right in and everybody loved the children. Alex even made the effort to learn some Portuguese and a bit about Brazilian culture.

My family was doing very well by then. My mother was living in a better house with a proper toilet, shower, electricity and a television. It had everything. My brothers and sisters had their own houses and the younger generation were all going to school and college, instead of having to work – they had dreams like the ones I had at their age. The village had moved on – into the 21st century. My oldest brother, Antonio, had even given up drinking. My mother put a special powder on his food and, if he drank alcohol, he felt really ill. He didn't know what she was doing and believed it was a sign from God. He never drank again.

Life returned to normal when we arrived back in England and I didn't want it any other way. *Normal* was great. I was still working, but we could afford an au-pair to look after the house and children. Alex became a manager with Thames Water and he was earning very good money. He was drinking a lot and sex was still an issue with me, so we both had our hang-ups. But the house was peaceful and what couple is ever perfect? If we could be sometimes happy and frequently content, that was all we could reasonably ask for.

We travelled to Scotland to see his family every three months and went on regular holidays abroad and Alex bought his first new car. We also agreed that I should go back to Brazil to visit my family once a year and not be away from them as much as I had been in the past.

The next time it was just me and the children who went – Alex couldn't come with us because of commitments at work. I was sorry to leave him with Gemma and our au-pair, but I believed he would be alright. He loved Gemma and he always treated the au-pairs like his own daughters. I went for three weeks and stayed with my brother, Dirceu. I telephoned Alex every day and he seemed very pleased to hear from me – for the first week. By the second week, there was something in his voice that wasn't quite right. The third week, he didn't pick up the phone. I was worried in case something had happened to him, but there was nothing I could do. We only had mobile phones, not a landline, so I couldn't ring the au-pair to find out if anything was wrong.

When we got back, Alex met us at Heathrow airport. He looked grim-faced and I knew something wasn't right. I asked him what was the matter and why he didn't answer my calls, but he said there was nothing wrong and that he was busy at work and had his phone switched off most of the time. The gentle Alex was gone and this sullen man had replaced him.

Things got bad between us. Alex started spending all his evenings in front of the computer. He either gave me the silent treatment or was shouting and swearing about one thing or another. Sometimes when he looked at me, it was like he was a stranger – almost as if he was possessed – like there was some kind of bad spirit inside him. The old angry Alex was back again.

There was another side to Alex's life that I knew nothing about. He was taking drugs – I don't know how long for, or why. I don't know what kind of drugs he was taking or where he got them, and I don't want to know. Maybe it was down to the sexual side of our marriage and, if so, then it was my fault. Maybe it was pressure at work, maybe it was his reserved personality, maybe it was his drinking that led him into it. I don't know because he wouldn't tell me. I found a packet of white powder and I was angry because the children could have found it. When I confronted him, he said it wasn't his, but I knew it was, because it had changed him. He became a different person – not when he was taking the drugs, but when he wasn't taking them.

I knew about cocaine from my time in Cracolândia and I knew the drug destroyed people's lives – it destroyed whole families as well as individuals.

I tried everything in my power to understand Alex, to help him. I asked him to go to rehab, but he would deny he was taking anything and get angry with me. Over the next few years, things got worse. Life became a living hell. From the moment Alex entered the front door, peace would fly out the window. I became scared of him, something I had never been before. He wasn't physically violent – he was never that – but the psychological torture was just as bad. The worst thing of all was that I don't believe he was even aware of what he was doing.

If a woman is beaten by her partner, she has the marks on her body to prove it happened, even if only to herself. With psychological violence, there's nothing to show and you begin to doubt yourself – your sanity.

'I want to show you something.'

He would call me over to the computer and show me gruesome acts of cruelty on internet sites. I didn't know much about the internet at that time and I don't know what websites he was looking at – but he would call me, no matter where I was in the house.

'Rozana, come look at this.'

They were graphic descriptions of how to kill people in the most brutal and cruel ways and they made me sick. I couldn't watch them and I don't know why he did. I felt threatened by it and didn't know how or why it would amuse him.

Once, Alex came home and he didn't say anything, just looked at me in a weird way. I didn't sleep that night because I was afraid he was going to kill me. But how could I tell anyone that? If I went to the police, they'd think I was mad and have me committed to a mental hospital. It got to the point where I couldn't cope with the situation any longer and I asked Alex to divorce me. As far as he was concerned, there was nothing wrong with our marriage and he refused. I threatened to run away and take the children with me. He said if I left him, he would find me – anywhere in the world.

I believed he would – and he'd kill me.

I was never a very good cook so, trying to make things better between us, I got a job as a catering assistant. The pay was less than I was earning before, but my boss, Louise, was a brilliant chef and she taught me how to cook properly. I thought this would please Alex. Before, we were living on steak and potatoes, or tinned food, ready meals and sandwiches. Now I was serving up a different delicious meal every day, but I don't think he even noticed.

Alex never took any drugs in front of me or the children, but sometimes he would be in such a bad state that he wouldn't eat or sleep for days. Then he'd stay in bed for twenty-four hours, get up and be alright for a while – until it started over again.

I was losing all hope. I was getting sick because I was afraid he would snap some day and do something bad to me or the children. He started to criticise everything I did – there was no doing right by him. I forgot what it was like to be happy and my state of mind reverted to when I was younger in Brazil – I was a bad person and everything was my fault. I could see no way out – no future. I was anxious and nervous all the time and lost all of my self-confidence.

The darkness came back.

Again.

CHAPTER NINETEEN
BUSINESS

Things got so bad that every time the doorbell rang, I thought it was the police, coming to tell me Alex had overdosed on some substance, or he had been arrested and was languishing in jail. I hated myself for having such negative feelings, but I couldn't help it.

Let me say this categorically: Alex never believed or understood that what he did hurt me. Had he realised, I feel sure things would have been different. It's probably my fault for not expressing myself properly, but there are times when life becomes a matter of survival, inside your head, when you are too hurt to care about other people. Instead, you just concentrate on yourself and your children. I was beginning to believe in my heart, if we were to have any hope of happiness – myself and the children – it would have to be without Alex. All the love I had for him was ebbing away.

I'm sure it was the same for him. I'm sure he felt I hated him because I couldn't understand him and wouldn't have sex with him. I couldn't blame him if he believed that. Blame is something people do when they are hurt. They lash out at each other and it's not something I want to do now. If there were things to blame, then it was my unreasonable neurosis after Julia's birth, my erratic hormones and my impossible assumptions that everything could be perfect in life. Also to blame was the person or persons who introduced Alex to drugs – who convinced him that was the answer to his problems. But I'm past all that now – blame and bitterness and accusation and anger.

All I had left were my children and my instincts. When I say "instincts," I really mean my faith – and when I say "faith," I don't mean a belief in any particular deity. I mean something inside me – an "old soul" telling me that bad news isn't always bad at all; telling me things will come good in the end. This faith was always there, even in the bad moments. Even when I didn't recognise it.

Luckily, nothing bad happened to Alex, despite my heart-searching and hoping. He didn't have a drink-driving accident, or get arrested at work for smoking marijuana, or accidentally burn down the house. As a matter of fact, instead of continuing on a downward spiral, our relationship made one last attempt at survival.

Just before Christmas 2008, the Alex I loved came back for a brief while – the beautiful man I first met in that park in Dagenham, the person I fell in love with and dreamed of spending the rest of my life with.

Alex's natural father, Jamie, asked us to spend Christmas with him in the north of Scotland. Both of us were sceptical of each other at first, but reluctantly agreed it would be good for the children to meet their real grandfather for the first time in his new home in Scotland.

I liked Jamie a lot, he was an atheist in his fifties, but very positive in his outlook on everything. He had overcome cancer in his early thirties and was very philosophical about life. He was married again to a woman called Jo, who was Italian. She was quite a shy person but very welcoming, and I got along great with her.

Alex and his father hadn't spoken to each other for years, so this was a kind of reunion; a reconciliation for both of them. I think it may have been part of Alex's problem. I don't believe he ever felt loved, even by me, or that he really belonged anywhere.

Jamie's house was large and the village near Inverness was small, with mountain views to the front and woods with a clearwater spring at the back. It was very picturesque and I fell completely in love with the place. After so long of living like strangers, Alex and I went for walks in the woods together and took the children sledging in the snow. We even climbed the hills that hovered over us.

After Christmas dinner, we sat by a roaring fire and played monopoly and drank wine and laughed together and it was beautiful. Alex could see me again, and I could see him. We were happy in the magical surroundings. Alex felt he belonged somewhere at last, even if it was temporary – transient. We were in the moment – and the moment was good.

When the children went to bed, we left Jamie and Jo enjoying wine by the fire and went for another walk – just the two of us. It was snowing heavily and the evening had a strange sort of luminescence. The enchanted half-light danced through the trees like flitting faeries, hiding from us and filling the wood with an air of mysticism. We felt like Hansel and Gretel, searching for our salvation. You would think this was an ideal time to talk about our problems, but that was something we never did. Alex would never admit he had problems and if I tried to speak about anything serious, he would change the subject.

So we pretended everything was alright.

Alex did promise that 2009 would be different though, so we went home for the new year and had a bit of a party with friends from London and Hertfordshire. When everyone was gone, we sat together on the sofa, hugging and promising each other that from then on, things would only get better. I was so tired after the long day, when I went to bed I fell asleep as soon as my head touched the pillow. Alex didn't come with me – he never went to bed before 2:00am.

I was soon awoken by an urgent knocking on the bedroom door. Startled, I noticed Alex wasn't lying beside me.

'Who is it?'

'It's Miria.'

Miria was our au-pair. I jumped out of bed, thinking something was wrong with the children. Miria was crying when I opened the door.

'What is it? What's wrong?'

'Mr Alex . . .'

'What about him?'

'He came into my bedroom.'

She said Alex tried to have sex with her. I couldn't believe it. Maybe he just went into the wrong bedroom. It *had* to be a mistake. I found him downstairs with his head in his hands. He wasn't with it at all. I felt sure he was on something, but I didn't know what.

'Did you go into Miria's room?'

'I must have.'

'Don't you know?'

'No. Yes! I did something.'

'Why?'

'I don't know why.'

His head stayed down and he wouldn't look at me. Then he stood up and left the house, right in the middle of the night.

I couldn't believe what had happened. If it had been before Christmas, I would have understood, but we were back together and had just promised one another things would be different. I began to blame myself. Maybe I should have waited for him and we should have gone to bed together. I should have been more encouraging and not so tired.

Alex slept in the car that night, but I couldn't sleep at all.

The next morning he was too embarrassed to talk about what happened. He packed a bag and went to stay with one of his friends. It didn't make sense to me. Just as we were about to function normally again, we'd gone and destroyed it through carelessness.

I tried to talk to Miria.

'What actually happened, Miria?'

'I don't know. It's a blur.'

'What did he do?'

'I can't remember.'

Or she didn't want to remember.

Miria left after a couple of days and went back to Brazil. The whole episode was obviously my fault because I didn't want sex. Alex was trying to control himself, but every man has his breaking point and after the drinks of the New Year's Eve party –

Alex came back to talk to me a few days later, but he was completely out of it on something. I can't say if it was alcohol or something else, but he made no sense. I could see he was really sorry for whatever it was he did, but could not understand why he'd done it. He didn't blame me, even though I was surely the one to blame. I had no idea how to feel. I was so disappointed we had lost the chance to get back together and now Alex was either drinking or taking drugs again. I felt defeated, worn down, like it was never going to be any different between us.

Alex kept coming back every day. It was a horrible situation. It was winter and he would stand in the garden and the children would cry and ask me to let him in. And I would. It was like he was living with me, but not living with me. He was like a walking contradiction. Did he want to be a husband, a father and a family man, or did he want to be footloose and free to drink with his friends and do whatever he wanted?

To be honest, I don't think he really knew what he wanted.

Separating from a partner is difficult enough when it's a clean break, because you have to deal with your own emotions and explain the situation to the children and sort out your finances. In my case it was more difficult because Alex kept turning up at the door every day and making it impossible to move forward.

I didn't know where I stood.

He stopped going to work and followed me about, just as he did with Sharon before me. After a few weeks he lost his job and it was down to me to support myself and my children. I don't know if not going to work was the only reason for Alex losing his job, or if there were other reasons as well. Maybe he wanted to lose it. He never really confided much about his private life. When his money ran out he would sleep in the car outside the house, or I would come home from work and he would be asleep on the sofa. This went on for months, until he met a woman called Marcia and moved in with her.

I was working full-time and had a new au pair called Andrea, but the money I earned as a catering assistant wasn't nearly enough to pay the mortgage and everything else as well. That's where the cooking skills I'd learned from Louise came to my aid. I gave up my full-time job and began to work as a sous chef for a different company. The wages were much better, but still not enough to pay all the bills.

I had some things in the shed, old clothes and stuff. A friend of mine had a car and we took it all to a car-boot sale, where I made £180. I bought a small vacuum cleaner, a bucket, a mop and some cleaning products, then I had leaflets printed up, advertising myself as a house cleaner. I delivered them by hand from door to door in the more affluent areas of West Hertfordshire.

I got some responses and I worked as a sous chef in the morning from 7:00am until 1:00pm before cleaning houses in the afternoons and evenings. Sometimes I didn't get home until 10:00pm. I really hated being away from my children so much, but I had no choice. I didn't want to go on benefits because I had worked all my life and wanted to continue to do so. I managed to make a bit of money and bought myself a little second-hand Astra car for £300, which made things a lot easier.

I kept on cleaning houses for about a year. I was self-employed and I went to a company called Hillier Hopkins to get myself an accountant. They advised me that there was more money to be made in corporate cleaning and, as a matter of fact, they needed a cleaner for their own offices. I was always a good worker and, while I was in catering, I was employed by corporate organisations that were suddenly asking me to quote for their cleaning contracts. Having a prestigious client like Hillier Hopkins gave me a good starting reference and some of the others followed suit.

I had to attend an interview for one of the contracts, which was worth a lot of money to me. There were three executives in the office and after interrogating me, they told me they had quotations from other cleaning companies.

'What makes you different from the others?'

My English wasn't perfect at the time.

'The most important thing is, I will never rape you.'

I meant to say "I will never rip you off."

'That's very reassuring.'

I got the contract.

As Alex and I were split up, Gemma went back to her mother when she was fourteen. Alex saw Julia and Callum on weekends and had his own life and relationships – the children always loved him dearly and looked forward to seeing him. He was working again and things had got back to some kind of normality.

Once I had a solid client base, I started a limited company called Right Option Cleaning and registered it with Companies House. With corporate cleaning, you don't get paid until the end of the month. This meant that cash flow was always a problem to begin with and there were times when I struggled to stay afloat. I put long hours and a lot of hard work into the business and it grew. I was lucky too, and with some very good and loyal clients I expected to turn over £35,000 in my first year. In actual fact, I turned over £100,000 and, thanks to that, I was able to keep up with my mortgage and all the other expenses.

Once I felt safe with the company, I left my sous chef job and invested all my time and energy into the business. Within two years, I was dealing with international companies and I had a secretary and an administrator to help me out on the legal side of things. I began to employ cleaners to do the work I was doing on my own, but I still wasn't afraid to get my hands dirty if I needed to. I always employed local people when I could and paid above average wages.

I've been trading for over six years now and, if I wanted to, I could probably be turning over a lot of money – but I chose to keep it small. I never had anything in my life and I once believed happiness and money were the same thing. They're not, I realise that now. The bigger the business, the less time I would have to spend with my children, who are all-important to me. I have some very good clients, I employ about forty people and instead of spending all my time working, I live my life lightly and do the things I really want to do. I'm now in my mid-forties and I feel better than I ever have in my life. I'm not on any medication and the depression is gone completely.

I still don't understand why it came, or how it went. I just know it's gone and it will never come back. I'm a different woman now than I ever was before. My children are the most precious things in my life and I still go visit my family in Brazil every year. I have lots of English and Brazilian friends who are always there for me and who encourage and support me. I look on my life now as a gift from my mother and father. It didn't come with an instruction manual and I made many mistakes on my way through it. But I learned from those mistakes and my struggles have given me the power to overcome my limitations and take responsibility for the things that happen to me; to rise above them and progress to the next level of who I am and who I will be.

It was never easy, but it was always worth it.

I still write my street poetry. I call it "street poetry" because that's precisely where it comes from. It's a stream of consciousness that invades my thoughts when I'm in a vacant mood. It's like graffiti of the mind and it says things to me that aren't always immediately comprehensible.

I believe poetry – at least, modern poetry – is inspired by sadness. It was for me and, sometimes, it still is.

Then I got the urge to write something else, a testimony – a witness statement – maybe even a confession, to exorcise myself from some of the demons still inside me. And so I wrote this book, not because I wanted people to think I suffered a lot, or how great I was for overcoming all of my trials. I just wanted to get it out of me and onto a page so I could look at my life objectively and become familiar with it in a way that wasn't painful. Then somebody said it would make a good book because it could be an inspiration to others who might be troubled or doubting themselves in some way.

Perhaps it will. Perhaps it won't. I don't know.

It just is what it is.

What I would really like to do is pass on this simple message – wherever your dream is, there is a map inside your heart with the way to get there. The road for me to get where I am now – both physically and emotionally – was very long, and many times I felt like giving up. But I never did. I followed the map in my heart, even when I seemed completely lost and there was no way forward. I kept going because, even if it was in the wrong direction, it was better than standing still.

When I was a child, my dream was to have food every day. When I was older, it was to go to school. When I became a teenager, it was to have nice clothes and a boyfriend. In my twenties, it was a car and my own flat and to go to expensive nightclubs. Until recently, it was to be married to a good man and have a family with a nice house to live in. In a way, I've achieved all those things at one time or other, but my dreams haven't always stayed with me. Nevertheless, I am as happy now as I could reasonably wish to be. My dream now is for my children to be happy, to enjoy the sunshine in summer, the wind in winter and the rain on the days in between.

CHAPTER TWENTY
STREET POETRY

I still love poetry. Unlike when I was younger, my street poetry now has no meter or rhyme. It's prose poetry, I suppose, relevant to my life, my past and my present and my future – and the way I think. It's sometimes oblique and may be difficult to understand, or maybe not. Like all poetry, it's extremely personal and maybe other people won't see it clearly – the sentiments or the meaning. If there is meaning.

Like when I was in Cracolândia, I watched the poor people and realised that there are many windows in the wall. Some see love, some see hate, some see life and others see death. Everybody chases their own dragon. Everybody wants Heaven / Nirvana / Eden / Valhalla / Elysium / Avalon. To transcend the world for even a few minutes is a longing of the soul. People don't chase their dragon because they want to be bad – they do it because they want to escape. Sanity and sobriety will only take them so far. After that it must be religion – or death.

The way to consciousness is through subconsciousness and the way to subconsciousness is through the chemistry of the mind. We're made up of those chemicals – we *are* those chemicals. It's just a matter of control and understanding. Some may say bad can't be good, no matter how you phrase it. Perhaps not – but to become good, we have to admit that we're bad.

They say life is sacred, but some lives aren't sacred at all. They're quick and ignominious and brutal and misunderstood. Yet they have to be lived. They're part of what we call being, for want of a better definition. Part of everything. And everything that lives moves – or seems to:

> *Nothing is constant.*
> *Nothing can be depended upon to remain.*
> *Some things I would like to remain and others I would like to change.*
> *It can't be both ways.*
> *Everything is transient.*
> *Yet time itself does not really move.*
> *Only we, by our choices, move through the infinite worlds of a future that already exists and a past that's always been there.*
> *And the fear of life is just as real as the fear of death.*
> *For some people.*

So, perhaps you can see how this street poetry comes upon me rather than to me? It's not like some kind of divine revelation. It's subtler than that, creeping up on me when I'm at my most contemplative. It's not something I ask for or seek out. It's part of the "old soul" within me – a kind of intuition seeping out of it and into me. Intuition, like knowledge, is power, and to deny that intuition would be to deny myself the power of expression. It would keep me psychologically weak; intellectually incompetent.

Believing I'll be rewarded for ignorance and superstition in the next life, or the one after that, or the one after that – it's a lie. Some say a little knowledge is a dangerous thing, but complete ignorance is a crime. I must drink from the Pierian spring to know truth, and truth is not absolute. It's multiple and contradictory, either known or not known. And a thought, once created, is as real as an electron – or a stone.

It's indestructible.

In my opinion, it's fragmented egoism that denies insight. Do we begin as nothing and end as nothing? What about the bit in between? Why do some people sail so easily through a soft little life, while others struggle and suffer? Where's the fairness? Where's God? Reincarnation?

No. Still not fair. One series of lives will never be identical to another. The answer is in the oneness – one plus one plus one plus one equals one. Everyone is everyone. But how can that be? It's easy:

> *I try to lift the clouds from my horizon and realise that I'm everyone.*
> *Everyone who ever lived and everyone who will ever live.*
> *If I understand that, I understand everything.*
> *I understand that love is the only way forward.*
> *If I love and help someone, I love and help myself.*
> *If I hate and harm someone –*

When I was young, I saw that hunger was intimidation and usually accompanied by prejudice and hypocrisy. The human condition, with its silhouettes for which there's no responsibility and its senses for which there's no adequate control, is steeped in the animal. Except the animal has no mechanism for conscience – no facility for remorse. The animal is blameless in its barbarity. The human is not:

> *What does it gain me if my avarice destroys everything around me?*
> *If I gain the whole world, yet lose that sense of propriety that lifts me above the animal – my humanity.*
> *Human.*
> *Being.*
> *And being cannot be separated from becoming.*

I know I'm capable, at any moment, of seeing all. It's only my brain that blocks it out, to save my sanity. And someone once told me that sanity is only the narrowsafe perception of a blinkered existence.

When I was young, I wanted to be educated. I longed for understanding. I longed to know. I needed answers to my many questions. If the answers weren't the ones I wanted, maybe they were the ones I needed. I confused love with longing. Longing is desire and desire destroys. There's always a price to be paid for longing. Sometimes the price is worth it and sometimes it isn't. Sometimes what you pay for is not what you intended to buy, just a sentimental substitute. And sentiment is something that belongs to other people and they loan it to you because they like the way you look or the way you fuck. But they always want it back in the end. One way or another. And it turns sour and leaves the bad taste of regret in your mouth – like a lie. Real understanding comes when you escape from the world of small self and the moral and opinionated and assertive. When you realise how minute the ego is against the backdrop of everything.

Only knowledge can recognise truth – real truth. And truth creates more knowledge. Here's how it seems to me sometimes:

When I look towards the light,
do I see the glow of realization,
the purity of perception,
or just the glare of confusion,
without shadow or relief – ubiquitous and implacable?
If meaning is menacing,
if it's hell,
then is it a hell of my own making?
Life itself is daunting – short and indiscriminate.
I feel as if I've been wandering in the desert,
shunned by society,
misunderstood, despised, discriminated against,
and I go from God to God until they cry from me in me –
O thou I!

The bread I eat is only mine when no one else wants it.
Life isn't there for personal gratification.
I must look at the light, even if I can't bear it – the glare.
I must look until I understand.
Look at it until it blinds me – until I'm so blind I can see.

There.

You see how this street poetry comes to me? How it manifests itself, like butterflies fluttering inside my head. I don't blame you if you can't understand it, but I wanted to write this chapter because it's part of me and to leave it out would be to write something incomplete. Neglected in some way. Defective.

I was brought up as a Catholic in Brazil, apart from the time when I was a Mormon. Now the God of my childhood is a stranger to me. I no longer ask who made God – I ask who makes God. Who makes God is God. The sun was once God – and still is. I was my own creator – of God and time, and I wore both like a ball and chain – measured them and carried them with me, but they were illusions. I needed to recognise what I was seeing and what I was not seeing.

Back in Brazil, the old people had this saying: "*There is a rock one mile high; one mile wide and one mile deep and a small bird comes every hundred years to sharpen its beak. When the rock is gone – has been worn away – then I may begin to see*".

That makes sense to me now:

Sometimes my body feels as if it's closing in on itself, growing denser;
more tightly packed.
Like a piece of condensed clay.
Like something that can be held in the hand and squeezed.
Packed tighter and tighter.
Crushed.
Ground down smaller and smaller.

Not human anymore.
Inhuman.
The quantum and the quark.
That's me – and my God.

Some things are difficult to understand and some things are simple. The spider kills the fly and the bird kills the spider and the dog kills the bird and the pig kills the dog and I kill the pig and the invisible micro-organism kills me. Full circle! We're not what we seem to be, just a mass of microbes and bacteria and DNA strings. We're capable of being broken down to the sub-atomic level, where nothing is what it seems to be:

Only the soul is what it seems to be.
And the soul is love.
Indivisible, like an idea; a concept; a dream.
This does not need to be learned.
It's already there.
It just needs to be understood – to overcome the rational,
dualistic mind and lead to the unifying ground of an existence
shared by all.
To understand how to achieve contentment in the midst of
a complicated, materialistic world – not how to escape that
world and all its problems.
I must live to be able to die.
I must die to be able to live.
And understanding will only come if it's called.

So you see, in my street poetry, life is like breaking a person down to their most basic level and putting them back together again. What comes back is not what went in. Bits are missing or added or changed about. The same ingredients, but a different person, looking for a place that was once known, in the remote future:

> *If there was a beginning, was there a beginner?*
> *Ex Nihilo.*
> *Genesis.*
> *Big Bang or Moment of Creation?*
> $E = MC^2$.
> *Ratio of matter/energy to volume/space at moment of bang/*
> *creation = one quadrillionth of one percent of ideal.*
> *Miraculous?*
> *A little matter – a lot of energy.*
> *Or is it all just an elaborate practical joke?*

That's what I mean by streams of consciousness. Strange, eh?

I read somewhere that the cosmos is expanding and the spaces between galaxies are getting bigger and bigger, moving further and further apart. To end up as a great cold dead graveyard when all the stars burn themselves out. Or maybe gravity will reverse it and everything will contract inwards until the universe is as big as a tennis ball, so dense and hot it will implode into the ultimate black hole. Either way, what will be there then, in the space left behind? Will it regenerate into something else – reinvent itself, as we do?

I know this will sound like me preaching, and it's not meant to. I'm no preacher and I don't wish to convert anyone to anything. But nothing can be taken for granted. Anything can occur in the turmoil of life. It's like a battlefield, and every soldier believes death will visit the next man, not him – otherwise he would never fight. Many die unprepared. We need to use our time wisely. If we've done nothing with today, it's because we believe we have many more days. We believe we can spare one, or two, or a hundred. We waste our time on nothing, on things that don't matter:

What if tomorrow were to be the final day of life?

Would we waste today?
Many pretend they're preparing, but few are ever prepared.
There are dangers around every bend in the road,
behind every tree in the forest,
in every man's smile,
in every woman's eyes.
The danger is everywhere.
It is constant.
It makes us lose touch with language and love and logic and life.
And the psychotic wall gets higher,
so high it will be impossible to ever break out.
The terminal isolation of insanity looks over the wall.
And says "suicide."
Carve your failure in stone!

When I was in the forest with the old *Curandeiro*, I heard that strange music – that musical note, played on a guitar string – the note I followed, trying to fathom its symmetry; its meaning. To me, music is the purest form of art. It takes me above all earthly things, all mundane matters. It's like being high. It is high. Sometimes I hear that same musical tone and I know I'll never understand that sound as I understood it back then. Sometimes it begins quietly, like a ghost tiptoeing through a forest. Then it becomes louder. Darker. Louder. Darker. Huge. Overpowering and intimidating. So loud it almost blows my mind apart. Then it quietens again, becoming slow and sad, occupying my complete concentration. I try to write it into my poetry and it comes out something like this:

I could lie down like a tired child and weep away the life of care I have borne and yet must bear till death, like sleep, might steal on me.
And will I hear that music after I am dead?

Softwhispering.

Sometimes the nights are long and the days are longer, even with the sky eye-blue above. My mind craves some kind of mooring and that's when I write the street poetry. Here's a recent one about the depression I suffered from for a lot of my life:

My life is adrift on a rapid river of uncertainty, rushing headlong to hell.
Faces flash past me – white – black – young – old.
Familiar feelings return – not felt for some time – but back now.
Despair. Disgust. Hatred. Apathy. Love. Life. Death.
All come close in the dark-light.
And I know I will dream the end of the dream I began, all that ancient time ago – all through the long minutes and days and years.
And I pretend for a while, until it all falls away and I am alone.
I know the nightmare will be re-dreamed, over and over again – until it becomes reality.
My mouth opens and closes, but no words emerge.
I am drowning in the depression.
One face keeps coming back into my head and the mouth keeps opening and closing and the eyes keep pleading and the soft soul keeps crying – its little heart out.

Another one I wrote after dreaming about when I was born. In the dream, I could feel myself emerging from the womb and into the world. It was an amazing experience, even if it *was* only a dream. If it was a dream:

I have seen the fall from Eden.
I know the real trauma of that forgotten moment, when man

stepped out of the quantum wave and into time.
The sky was full of fire.
The fundamental forces of nature were all around.
I was part of all things.
The reality I observed was altered by the act of observation
and I had to choose my own path through the forest of photons
that flowed into me.
Filled me.
Became me.

Then I think I'm finished, but more comes on the heels of what came before:

And now I can stand naked in the universe and shout, "I know
that I know!"
Now.
Now, despite everything being relative, I know the beginning
of life is at the moment of conception, not the moment of birth.

Death is always a theme that recurs in my street poetry, probably because death was such a visible thing when I was young, such a ubiquitous thing, not hidden away and disguised as it is in more developed countries – but always close by:

Most people do not die – they are killed.
On street corners. In cardboard boxes.
Scraping out dustbins.
Exploited.
Lied to by the callous and uncaring.
Scavenging scarecrows in barren wastelands and polluted
hinterlands – being robbed and lab-ratted and raped.
The real nature of Human?

The Catholics told us a lot about heaven and hell when I was young, but I never really understood what they were talking about. What is heaven? What is hell? Are either where I want to be? Deserve to be? Is one better or worse than the other?

Sometimes I believe only what I can see exists. Only what I can touch and feel, but there are always new things to deal with – time and strangeness and living each moment on the edge of eternity, paying the heavy price of awareness.

Is there such a thing as never? Or forever? Forever never – never forever. Are my fractured perceptions flawed? Does the past cease to exist as soon as my awareness moves beyond it? Or is it always there, like a ghost in the gloom? Does the present only matter because I'm inhabiting it now? Or is today no more real than yesterday? I lived in that place once, crouched in my corner. I watched the dark sky through the small window, high up in the wall. The moon was battered. Broken.

I've always believed that the mystery of life shouldn't be a problem to be solved, just a reality to be experienced – if there is such a thing as experience:

The pendulum clock continues to tick.
Sometimes I do not hear it.
Other times it sounds like a hammer striking an anvil.
Every tick is an exploding second, every tock a dying moment.

They say, fifteen billion years ago, space and time began. What was there before that? In another fifteen billion years it may all end. What will come after it? What will fill the space left behind; the time still to come? Does time exist at all, or is it just something we created when we began to measure it? Maybe everything really just *is*. That's all!

I hear the vibration of the universe and I call it love.

I want to go to it, need to go to it, need to dissolve in it.
It calls me home.
And nothing is lived, but everything is re-lived – in the same way that all events are interlinked with each other, are part of each other, become each other, die and reincarnate as each other.
And real love is the shedding of old feelings, emotions, longings, wants.
And the knowledge that there will be no more turbulence.

Sometimes the sky is like velvet.
Rippled.
I am alone underneath it.
Not alone – solitary, but not alone.
The air around me is golden.
Firelike.
And I feel the glow.
I feel the force – the longing to lose everything – every feeling.
Hate and happiness and frustration and fear and life and love and hope and the human thing.
The human thing.
Whatever it is.
All the things that it is.
I want to go away from the solitude, into the aloneness.
To find something.
What it is all about.
The end result.
The absolute absolute.
The is-ness.
To find the answer to the only question left.
Why?

As I've grown older, I've learned to take only what's needed, not what's wanted. I've learned to identify need. It takes discipline, control, to control desire – distinguish it from need. Nowadays, everything that's heard is the static of want. Want this and want that – want, want, want. All time is spent wanting, listening to the want static. But desire can only destroy, even if it pretends otherwise. And love – love! Sometimes I find it hard to say that word. But how else can I clear my clouded perceptions – blow away the fog of smallself – break the chains of language – destroy the ladder? If I do not, I might climb back down again:

Can I be something I was never meant to be?
Only if I find the still landscape with no dramas and no symbols.
I listen, but I hear nothing because there is nothing to hear,
and it is beautiful and appalling at the same time.
And truth is more than just a state of mind.
Just as love is more than just a state of blind.

Like I've said before, there's a tone somewhere. A musical modulation. All my street poetry is inherent in that one tone – like religion. I try to follow the sound, but it fades into the distance. Just the vibration is left. Maybe it's the sound of my soul, trying to break free and fulfil itself in an eternal present, not in a past that never was or a future that never will be. In many situations, there's something infinitely futile and presumptuous about speech and only action is appropriate.

But not always:

Sometimes words are all that's left.
Sometimes there's no other warmth, no other cold.
No other right or wrong.
No action.
No conflict.
Just consequences.

Of what is.
What was.
What will never be.
Between one thing and another.
Neither one thing nor another.
And life is like that – word-like.
Wraith-like.
An illusion.
Sometimes.
Most times.
A mirage.
A vision.
Anamorphic.
There but not there.
For all eternity.

That's when I feel the words – the poetry.

I've gained a lot in my life, but I've lost a lot too. Loss is a sad colour – the colour of melancholy. The loss of something once loved. Someone once loved. There's always a residue left over, a redolence, an essence that will never go away. Nonexistent. Ghostlike. Hypothetical. I know I can never be free of it – really free:

Light and laughter were the flowers and dreamscapes of
innocent wistfulness and the understanding that there was no
life apart from living.
And it was never enough to say the earth goes round the sun.
I had to ask why.
And the more I knew, the less I understood.

I realise this penultimate chapter will seem abstract and ambiguous, but it's an essential part of my story – part of me – who I was, who I am and who I will grow to be. I've tried here to give an essence of what my street poetry is, but that's not an easy task for me, because I don't fully understand it myself.

I'll leave this chapter now, with one final piece of poetry – a prose poem, as I call them, not having the technical knowledge to call them anything else, that was inspired by trying to look at myself objectively:

Bodyandsoul.
Singerandsong.
Beingandbecoming.
I am evolution made conscious of itself.
I am Gaia!
Hydrogenhuman.
Everyone I know will go and I will be left with the hostile strangers.
I will lose touch with language.
And love.
And logic.
And life.
No more change.
No more choice.
I am aware that the present does not exist
– so it cannot be now
– it can only be then.
Whose imagination am I a figment of?
There is more I need to ask
– things that have not been explained.
But there is no time left.
It is gone!

CHAPTER TWENTY-ONE
DENOUEMENT

My daughter Julia is fifteen now, and my son Callum is twelve. I still live in Hertfordshire and I still have my cleaning company. I am also a partner in an events management company and I'm still writing.

I have a cordial relationship with Alex, who has access to the children on weekends and holidays. I am still single, and I prefer it that way. My ideal partner would be a kind, handsome man with whom I could have a loving, semi-platonic relationship, without too much sex, but that's unlikely to ever happen. No matter, I can live with myself quite happily.

I love to visit my family in Brazil every year. They came from being the poorest family in the region to being one of the more affluent ones, and I hope I was influential in getting them to move forward. I'm no longer the black sheep – the prodigal daughter. My mother is still alive and living in Lageado. She discovered that her mother, my maternal grandmother, was called Taciana and she didn't speak Portuguese, but Ukrainian. My maternal grandfather was called Pedro, but nobody knows anything about him.

I have many close friends in Brazil who helped me over the difficult years. I will never forget them, but the UK is my home now. My life is here, with the people, with the winters, with my children.

Ricardo Siremarco is sixty-five now and he is my best friend, apart from Malu. He went on to be a very well known artist and even had an exhibition at the Tate Modern in London. I see him when he comes to England and when I go to Brazil. He has a house in the *Serra da Mantiqueira* with a studio where he likes to paint. If I ever retire, I would like to have a house in the mountains close to his, where I could go for solitude and inspiration.

Malu is my great friend, without her help I would never have survived. She will be my friend for life and I am deeply indebted to her. She does a lot of charitable work in Brazil and is truly a benevolent and spiritual woman.

Nisi married a millionaire and now lives in Singapore. I still have contact with her and we meet up whenever she comes back to England. Fabi is married and has two wonderful children and she runs her own business back in Brazil now. Abi is married to a lovely Irishman and has a beautiful daughter. She still lives in England and we meet up regularly. Jamie and Jo split up after thirty years and I have become best friends with her. Incidentally, we now work together.

Sex has always been an issue for me, probably because of the things that happened when I was young. It's difficult to talk about sometimes and maybe I need some kind of therapy. My particular image of the perfect woman has been tall, blue-eyed, blonde, white teeth – all the things I wasn't myself. After Alex, I didn't want another relationship – I didn't want a partner, nor did I want to have sex with anybody else. I preferred to be on my own. Then, in 2014, I saw Colette working in a coffee shop where I was conducting some business. She looked like a model who had just stepped from the pages of a fashion magazine. I had occasion to see her several times after that and she began to pay me compliments.

'I like your hair, Rozana.'

'Thank you, Collette.'

'We should go for a drink sometime.'

'Should we?'

'Yes, why not?'

So I went. After a few drinks, I was getting a bit tipsy and we were talking about lots of things. I told her about my breast reduction – I don't know why.

'Show me.'

'What, here?'

'No, not here.'

We went back to her flat and had some more drinks. It wasn't long before I was brave enough to show her my scars. One thing led to another and we began to undress each other. I didn't really know what I was doing, but I could feel her hands moving across my body, tempting me. She kissed my neck and down along my back. I tried to understand what was happening, it should have seemed unnatural – wrong – but it didn't. Saliva from her tongue trailed on my stomach and there was a sound inside my head, like water lapping up against a river's edge.

I can't remember much about what happened after that because it stole the time away from me like a thief. The experience was translucent. Hazy. Dreamlike. Soft sounds of pleasure. Strange words. Heat. Heartbeats.

For some reason, this experience opened my mind. After it, I began to find myself. I'd blocked out elements of my true nature and repressed many of my true feelings. That's not to say I realised I was gay – I was not. But for the first time, I saw that there were actually more things in heaven and earth than were previously dreamt of in my philosophy, to misquote Shakespeare. I realised I was squandering my life, throwing away minutes and hours and days and weeks and months – years. I'd begun to change.

Profoundly.

I had a butterfly tattooed on my stomach and this symbolised how I felt. I was, and am still, a free soul – and that's how I wish to remain.

This resolution was tested recently. I began trying to get fit, so I joined a gym – just to look and feel better and to stay healthy. I met a very good-looking guy there and we got on very well. I invited him round to my house.

'I can come this evening.'

He came and we had a drink and a chat and he left. Then he

texted me and asked to see me socially again. I started to have feelings for him, the kind of feelings I thought I would never have again. He came round again – and again – but there was nothing physical between us. One evening, he looked a little sad. I asked him what was wrong.

'I think you don't like me.'

'That's nonsense, Rozana.'

I thought maybe he wanted me to start things off, so I tried to kiss him. He pulled away.

'I can't do this.'

'Then why are you sad?'

'Because you're a friend. I like you. We have a laugh.'

He stood up and walked to the door.

'And . . . I'm married.'

Had this happened a few years earlier, it would have had a profound effect on my self-esteem, but now it didn't bother me. *C'est la vie*! I could move on immediately. That's when I knew I had changed.

I don't know what I was looking for with the man from the gym. Maybe I was testing myself, to see if I'd *really* changed and the old me was gone. To see if I still depended on other people's opinion of me – their affection for me – or lack of affection. You'll probably think it was reckless, and maybe you're right – maybe it was. But it was also a denouement, a confirmation to myself that the woman I'd always wanted to be – who I'd been waiting all these years to meet – was finally here.

So, that's where I am now. I am not in a relationship and it's fine. My businesses are doing very well and I have a wonderful rapport with my growing children and my ex-husband.

I think I would like to keep writing, maybe publish a book of street poetry or, if this book is well received, maybe I will write a fictional novel next – I have a good story in my head. I could maybe even make a Brazilian soap opera. That really would be extraordinary!

Whatever happens, I will go where life takes me. There is no secret to success in life, it's merely a series of situations and circumstance. It's being in certain places at certain times, whether right or wrong.

Somebody asked me recently if, given the choice, I would change the past? I had to think for quite a while, and my answer was, "probably not." The past is me. Everything I've experienced has contributed to who I am now. If I changed anything, I would be changing myself – and I don't want to do that. Finally, I am happy being who I am. Life will go on and I will continue to change and develop. In ten years' time I'm sure I will be an even different woman to the one I am today.

For better or worse, I look forward to meeting that woman.

AFTERWORD

When I first thought about writing this memoir, I wondered if people would want to read it. It's very dark in places and I worried that people wouldn't believe what I went through. Then I thought, what if there are other women out there going through what I went through – violence and intimidation – other girls suffering from depression and self-doubt? I believed my story could help them in some small way, maybe give them some help to move on, to keep going towards the light. It is there, at the end of the tunnel, believe me.

Once I'd established this belief in my mind, I came to the conclusion that my story was worth telling. Not in any presumptuous way, but just to write things down, to set the record straight, to come to some conclusions. I wanted to paint a picture of how the world is, to explain how things can change and be changed, with hope and determination.

Sometimes it's difficult to find the strength to move on. "What's the point?" I've often heard people say. There's *always* a point. Life is always changing, in a constant state of flux, and nothing stays the same forever. I realised a long time ago that feeling sorry for myself wasn't going to achieve anything. Nobody else was going to feel sorry for me and if I didn't like the way things were, I had to change them myself.

This book was also an exorcism of sorts for me – a way to purge the demons from my soul. It's been a liberating experience and one that I recommend.

But my main motivation was always to try to give people hope – to say to them, "You must not give up. You must find the courage to go on."

And, if you ever need someone to talk to, just give me a call.

Rozana

EPILOGUE
DISPARITY AND DISPAIR

In Brazil, the phenomenon of street children is caused by abandonment or the death of parents or family members. Street children live in abandoned buildings, cardboard boxes, parks or on the street itself. Most are between the ages of five and eighteen.

Once children are left on the streets, there's rarely any way back for them and life expectancy is very low. Estimates on the numbers of Brazilian street children vary from 200,000 to 8-million. They survive by salvaging food from rubbish bins and refuse tips or being exploited as shoe-shiners, thieves, prostitutes and drug runners.

Drug taking is common amongst street children in Brazil – particularly glue sniffing, as it's cheaper than the alternatives. Drugs help the children forget their life for a short time, but have a disastrous affect on their mental and physical health. They contribute greatly to the downward spiral of a child's life and can cause a child to become a virtual "zombie" as their mental functionality is increasingly impaired.

At best, most street children are viewed as a nuisance. At worst, they are an infestation that needs to be eradicated. Because they have no vote or voice, there's little impetus for the politicians to solve the issue. Any actions are so watered down by the time they get to street level that they become almost useless. Generally, jails are already full and apart from jail there are very few places children can be taken when picked up by the police. There are simply too many street children for the resources provided by the government to help.

Brazil is the fifth largest country in the world, with a population of approximately 190-million people. The disparity between the rich and poor in Brazilian society is one of the worst. The richest 1% of Brazil's population control 50% of its income. The poorest 50% of society live on just 10% of the country's wealth, while the poorest 10% receive less than 1%. Brazil also has the highest number of people living with HIV and AIDS in South America (estimated at 660,000). Prevalence is rising rapidly, and many people in need of treatment or care are excluded from services because of poverty.

Profound poverty means family disintegration and violence, meaning break-ups become more prevalent. The result is yet more street children.

As difficult as it is, I hope and pray the world will one day fix this cycle.

ACKNOWLEDGEMENTS

I would like to thank my family in Brazil, who were always there for me when I came limping home.

I would also like to thank my family in England, who are my whole reason for living.

My warmest thanks to all my friends, both in Brazil and Britain, who have coloured my life and made it the thing of beauty it is today.

And my grateful thanks to my professional colleagues, who always believed in me.

ABOUT THE AUTHOR

ROZANA McGRATTAN is a successful UK business woman who employs dozens of people in Hertfordshire, England, through her company **rightoptioncleaning.com**.

She has a wealth of experience in the marketing and promotional arenas, along with many contacts in the British and Brazilian media. This is her first book, but she has ambitions to write others on a variety of topics in both fiction and non-fiction.